WHAT IS YOUR I.Q. (Ice Quotient)?

Test it with these questions:

● Which National Hockey League player inadvertently "helped" Boston win the 1972 Stanley Cup by writing a chapter about the Bruins in his book?

● Can you name the man most responsible for making Jean Ratelle into a New York Rangers superstar?

● Why are there no blacks playing in the NHL?

● What was the turning point of the 1972 Stanley Cup final between the Rangers and the Bruins?

● Who invented and perfected goaltender's pads?

You may not be in the "hockey genius" category yet, but you will be after reading the answers to these and other questions in

HOCKEY STARS OF 1973

About the Author

STAN FISCHLER, author of a syndicated column, "Inside Hockey," also appears in *The Sporting News* where he writes "Speaking Out on Hockey." He has written numerous books including *Bobby Orr and the Big, Bad Bruins, Strange but True Hockey Stories,* and *Play the Man* (with Brad Park) among many others about hockey. He lives with his hockey-writing wife, Shirley; son, Benjamin; pet puli, Chazy; pet cats, Sybil and Max; and pet bird, Smedley, in New York City. Every so often he puts on the blades to prove he still has a lot to learn about hockey.

HOCKEY STARS OF 1973

STAN FISCHLER

Research Assistants
MIKE RUBIN
MIKE TROTT

PYRAMID BOOKS • NEW YORK

*To Toots, Who Provides The Foresight To Go
With My 20-20 Hindsight*

HOCKEY STARS OF 1973

A PYRAMID BOOK

First printing, October 1972

Copyright © 1972 by Stan Fischler

All Rights Reserved

ISBN 0-515-02831-2

Printed in the United States of America

Pyramid Books are published by Pyramid Communications, Inc.
Its trademarks, consisting of the word "Pyramid" and the portrayal
of a pyramid, are registered in the United States Patent Office.

Pyramid Communications, Inc., 919 Third Avenue, New York, N.Y. 10022

TABLE OF CONTENTS

Syl Apps, Jr.   Peter Mahovlich
Red Berenson   Johnny McKenzie
Yvan Cournoyer   Richard Martin
Ken Dryden   Stan Mikita
Phil Esposito   Bobby Orr
Paul Henderson   Brad Park
Bobby Hull   Jean Ratelle
Orland Kurtenbach   Walt Tkaczuk
Guy Lapointe   Mike Walton
Frank Mahovlich   Lorne "Gump" Worsley

THE OTHER HOCKEYS

SPECIAL BONUS SECTION

FOR a change logic prevailed in the National Hockey League race. The Boston Bruins, who finished the season on top of the East Division in 1971-72 with 119 points, romped to their second Stanley Cup world championship in three years.

Stopping the Boston hockey machine was like an ant trying to block a tank. The Bruins not only finished ten points ahead of their nearest foe, the New York Rangers, but also shellacked their traditional East Coast enemy in five out of the six games they played during the regular season and defeated New York four games to two in the Stanley Cup finals. Just to underline their total NHL superiority, the Bruins accumulated 14 more points during the regular season than the West Division champion Chicago Black Hawks.

"We came up with the best players ever assembled," said veteran Boston goalie Ed Johnston. "It was a great team because it won the big games; and it won the big games on the road."

The Bruins won the clinching Stanley Cup game on May 11, 1972, at Madison Square Garden, where they also defeated the Rangers in three-out-of-three regular season games during the 1971-72 season. "If we could get as high for the 78 regular season games as we did for that final game in New York," said Johnston, "we would have won them all."

Johnston's theory has some basis, judging by the Boston lineup. Defenseman Bobby Orr was named to the First All-Star Team, won the Norris Trophy as the NHL's best backliner, the Hart Trophy as the most valuable player, and the Conn Smythe Trophy as the best playoff performer.

Phil Esposito, the other half of Boston's one-two punch, led the league in scoring—Orr finished second—and was named First All-Star Center. Between them Bobby and Phil hypnotized the opposition just by stepping on the ice.

"Our team was awed by the Bruins," said St. Louis Blues coach Al Arbour, whose team was wiped out in four straight games of the Cup semifinals by Orr and Company. "We played in a trance; we were mesmerized. We saw Orr and Esposito out there and the rest of them and we wondered what we were doing playing on the same ice with them."

One theory had it that the Bruins could be deflated if Esposito's goal-scoring was neutralized and Orr's playmaking was contained. But this plan was exploded against the Rangers. Orr was hampered by an injured knee, yet managed to score the winning goal against New York in the Cup finale. Esposito didn't score a single goal against the Rangers in six playoff games but starred as a playmaker. "Esposito is a great hockey player," said Toronto Maple Leafs vice president King Clancy. "He plays the game both ways; he can kill penalties and if you stop him from scoring, he'll give the puck to someone else who'll score." Which is precisely what he did.

So glittering were the Bruins' individual and collective performances that they overshadowed outstanding teams elsewhere. The Rangers, for example, enjoyed a superb season led by All-Star defenseman Brad Park and the "Gag" (Goal-a-game) Line of Jean Ratelle, Rod Gilbert, and Vic Hadfield.

Until he was injured during the home stretch, Ratelle appeared to be a good bet to win the scoring championship. Although he missed 15 games, the lean New York center managed to score 46 goals and 63 assists for 109 points and finished third behind Esposito and Orr. Jean's reward was the Lady Byng Trophy for combining ability with good sportsmanship. "Ratelle," said Rangers general manager-coach Emile Francis, "is a perfect gentleman and a perfect hockey player."

Ratelle's linemate, Vic Hadfield, became the first Ranger ever to score 50 goals and finished the year in fourth place with 106 points while the line's third man, Rod Gilbert, was in fifth place with 43 goals, 54 assists, and 97 points. Injuries to each of the Gag line aces severely hampered their play in the Cup round. Ratelle was sidelined with an ankle injury as the Rangers defeated Montreal in the first playoff, four games to two, and went on to shellack Chicago in four straight games. Still hurting, Ratelle finally returned for part-time duty in the finals but was conspicuously ineffective.

Ratelle had an excuse but the even more conspicuously ineffective Chicago Black Hawks had no alibi for their abysmal 1972 playoff effort. Having run away with the West Division championship for the second year in a row, coach Billy Reay's Windy City skaters were regarded as a solid Cup threat.

But playing in the weaker West Division gave Chicago a distorted view of the power of the East. After sweeping Pittsburgh four-straight in the opening Cup round, the Hawks were thoroughly demolished by a Rangers team that was decimated by injuries. "I think our guys still were feeling the effects of the 1971 Cup defeat by Montreal," said coach Reay. But ex-Black Hawks ace Bobby Hull put the debacle in better perspective when he explained: "I think the coach was just trying to cover up for us. It just seemed that the Rangers wanted the win more than we did."

If Chicago emerged from the 1971-72 season with any consolation it was the fact that goalie Tony Esposito, playing in 48 games, had the best goals against average (1.76) in the league. The combination of Esposito and substitute Chicago goaltenders Gary Smith and Gerry Desjardins had a collective 2.12 goals against average to win the Vezina Trophy for the Black Hawks.

The next biggest disappointment, after Chicago's playoff failure, was the performance of the 1971 Stanley Cup champion Montreal Canadiens. Fortified with a new coach, Scotty Bowman, who supposedly would lead them to the top, the Canadiens never seemed able to squeeze themselves out of third place in the East and, most of the time, were saved by the heroics of goalie Ken Dryden who later was to win the Calder Trophy as "rookie of the year" although he had played briefly the previous season. "I was too easy on the team," Bowman explained. "Next season it will be different."

Bowman did obtain creditable performances from big left wing Frank Mahovlich, who finished sixth in scoring, and was heartened by the return of defenseman Serge Savard who had suffered a severe leg injury the previous year. It was expected that, although Montreal had played mediocre hockey during the regular campaign, the Canadiens would flash their "mystique" in the playoffs and skate to the finals. But Bowman discovered that the Canadiens' mystique was not retroactive and Montreal fell easy prey to the Rangers in six games.

One of the most exciting races of 1971-72 was for the fourth and final playoff spot in the East. The Detroit Red Wings, who dropped coach Doug Barkley and replaced him with Johnny Wilson early in the season, appeared capable of overtaking the Toronto Maple Leafs until Leaf coach ailing Johnny McLellan was sidelined with a nervous stomach late in the schedule. Just when it appeared the Leafs would collapse, ancient Hall of Famer King Clancy moved behind the bench and steered the Leafs into fourth.

"I used some good old Irish blarney to loosen them up," Clancy explained, "and some common sense."

Clancy led his Leafs against the powerful Bruins in the playoff opening series and startled the Bostonians with a sudden-death overtime win in the second game on a goal by center Jim Harrison. "With a break here or there," said Clancy, "we might have taken the series but we didn't get those breaks." The Bruins won the series in five games.

In the West Division, the most exciting playoff battle also was for fourth place when a three-way dogfight developed between the California Golden Seals, the Philadelphia Flyers, and the Pittsburgh Penguins.

The Seals, who late in the season traded their ace defenseman Carol Vadnais to Boston for Rick Smith, Ivan Boldirev, and Reg Leach, were dropped for the count when Boldirev was sidelined with mononucleosis in the stretch. That left the Flyers and Penguins to fight it out, and for some time it appeared Philadelphia would wrap up the remaining playoff prize.

All the Flyers needed was a win or tie in their last game of the season against Buffalo to take fourth, but a shot by Gerry Meehan of the Sabres beat Philadelphia goaltender Doug Favell with only four seconds of the final game remaining. The Flyers lost by a goal and Pittsburgh squeaked into fourth place.

Meanwhile the Minnesota North Stars, coaxing splendid seasons out of such old timers as Gump Worsley, Dean Prentice, Charlie Burns, and Doug Mohns, finished a solid second in the West, 19 points ahead of the third place St. Louis Blues. But age took its toll against the North Stars in the playoffs and the younger, speedier Blues upset Minnesota on Kevin O'Shea's dramatic sudden-death goal in the seventh game of the series.

The Blues then, unfortunately, went up against the Bruins in one of the most one-sided series in Stanley Cup history. Boston romped by embarrassing scores of 6-1, 10-2, 7-2, and 5-3 without even taking a second wind. In so doing the Bruins bombed three different St. Louis goalies—Jacques Caron, Ernie Wakely, and Peter McDuffe.

Boston's confrontation with New York was billed as a match-up made in heaven. The big bad Bruins were renowned for their roughhouse style that some observers claim has brutalized hockey. By contrast, the lighthorse Rangers were respected as a clean, short-passing team that stressed brains over brawn. An added fillip developed over a book, "Play the Man," authored by Rangers defenseman Brad Park.

In his book Park singled out such Bruins as Phil Esposito, Johnny McKenzie, and Ted Green for harsh criticism and thoroughly enraged the Beantown sextet before the opener. "You have to give Park credit," said Boston coach Tom Johnson. "His book helped us a lot whenever we played the Rangers. It gave our guys an extra incentive to beat them."

The series opened in Boston Garden on April 30, and for a time it seemed that Boston would run the Rangers right out of Massachusetts. The home team took a 5-1 lead only to see the New Yorkers rally to tie the score in the third period. But the Rangers couldn't capitalize on their momentum and Bruins utility forward Ace Bailey scored Boston's sixth and winning goal past Ed Giacomin at 17:44 of the third period.

When Boston won the second game of the finals, 2-1, some observers believed that Tom Johnson's sextet was capable of a playoff sweep but the Rangers, rallied by Park's two first-period goals in the third game, at Madison Square Garden, won the match, 5-2. Now, it appeared, the Broadway Blues might tie the series and stun the Bruins with an upset like the one the Canadiens perpetrated against Boston a year earlier.

But the Rangers, following their long-standing tradition, folded in the clutch. Giacomin gave up two goals to Orr and one to Don Marcotte in the vital fourth game before the Rangers could marshall an attack. Ted Irvine scored for the New Yorkers late in the second period and Rod Seiling got one late in the third but for the Rangers it was too little too late. Boston won, 3-2.

"That was the turning point of the series," said Boston goalie Gerry Cheevers who watched from the sidelines. "Our goalie, Eddie Johnston, made a big save on Vic Hadfield late in the second period when the Rangers had a power play and we took it from there."

Well, almost! The Bruins had hoped to wrap up the series at home on May 9 but they didn't reckon with little Gilles Villemure, Giacomin's understudy. Clearly the better of the two New York goalies over the regular season, Villemure came off the bench to play splendidly in the fifth game at Boston Garden. Meanwhile his mates rallied from 1-0 and 2-1 deficits to win on a pair of third period goals by little Bobby Rousseau, sending the teams back to Madison Square Garden for game six.

The finale was a viciously played game that saw Bobby Orr send Boston in front, 1-0, despite Villemure's acrobatics. The Rangers were unable to find the formula for beating Cheevers although they once enjoyed a two-man advantage in the second period. A pair of third-period goals by Wayne Cashman sealed delivery of the Stanley Cup to Boston and the Bruins skated off the ice with a convincing 3-0 win.

"Let's face it," said goalie Eddie Johnston, "we won every big game we had to win all season. That's the sign of a good club and that's why we won the Cup."

Perhaps Rangers captain Vic Hadfield had a more direct explanation of the playoff results, not to mention the story of the entire NHL season. "We played them pretty even," said Hadfield, echoing the sentiments of the other 12 Bruins opponents, "but they had Bobby Orr and we didn't!"

NOT long after his Boston Bruins had bashed and battered their way to a six-game Stanley Cup victory over the New York Rangers in the playoff finals, coach Tom Johnson reflected on what has become known as the big Bruins' bashing mode of hockey. "I guess," said Johnson, "our style is here to stay."

Crash-bam hockey as perpetrated by the Bruins has worked so well, has intimidated so many opponents and has escaped the eyes of referees so often that it appears to guarantee Boston another Stanley Cup in 1973—unless the New York Rangers, Boston's only genuine threat, can find an antidote to the Bruins' aggression.

At the moment this doesn't seem possible. Recent history has proven that no team in the National Hockey League can trade bodychecks and roughhouse play with the Beantowners and come out on top. It was vividly demonstrated last spring when the Bruins turned their beef on the smaller Rangers. "The real key to the series," said Boston defenseman Bobby Orr, "was the way we went at them in the games we won in New York. We went out and hit them and that turned the series around."

With such heavyweights as Don Awrey, Wayne Cashman, Ken Hodge, and Johnny Bucyk to maraud the enemy, the Bruins' stickhandling artists, including Phil Esposito and Fred Stanfield, are able to romp unmolested through the enemy lines. Then there is the all-purpose Orr. "He is," says Rangers general manager-coach Emile Francis, "one of the greatest players our game has ever seen."

Although the Bruins roster was slightly stripped around the edges by the WHA and the draft, which supplied talent to new franchises in Atlanta, Georgia and Long Island, New York, Boston has retained the nucleus of a 1973 Cup-winning powerhouse.

In a minor key, the same tune can be sung about the Rangers. Armed with such aces as defenseman Brad Park,

who in certain hockey skills is superior to Orr, center Walt
Tkaczuk and right wing Bill Fairbairn, the Rangers'
gravest weakness has been on left wing. Tommy Williams,
rookie of the year last season in the Central League, is a
top candidate for that spot.

A question mark for the New Yorkers is the ability of
crack center Jean Ratelle to regain his high-scoring form
after his ankle injury of March 1972. The impressive
development of Tkaczuk in the 1972 playoffs could give
the Rangers better punch down the center than the Bruins. "Tkaczuk can really zing the puck," said Boston goalie
Ed Johnston, "and he has a fast delivery. But he's big and
extremely strong, so he does the sort of thing Phil Esposito does for us. He barges right into the goalmouth."

If Francis can produce a suitable left wing to complement Tkaczuk, and Ratelle regains his 1971-72 form, the
Rangers will have the firepower to go with their motiva-
tion—they haven't won the Stanley Cup in 33 years nor
finished first in 31 years—and just might reach the NHL
pinnacle.

After New York and Boston, only Montreal looms as a
potential threat in the East. With one full season under his
belt, Calder Trophy winner Ken Dryden could provide the
Canadiens with the best netminding in the East. If he
does, and Frank Mahovlich and Yvan Cournoyer score
the way they did last year—a total of 90 goals—Montreal
will have a shot at the top if one other young man comes
through.

The potential ace in question is none other than Guy
Lafleur, the sophomore who entered the league last season
on an avalanche of press clippings but who produced in
eminently nonspectacular fashion. If Lafleur can lift his
scoring average to a-point-a-game—last year he scored 64
points in 73 games—and improves on his drive and defensive play, Montreal could surprise the Big Two.

Certainly it would *not* be a surprise to see the Detroit
Red Wings overtake the Toronto Maple Leafs in the
challenge for fourth place in the East. Effervescent coach
Johnny Wilson has molded a speedy, galvanic Motor City
team spearheaded by sophomore ace Marcel Dionne, fleet
Mickey Redmond, and promising young defenseman Ron
Stackhouse. If the Detroiters can mend the holes in their

goaltending armor they will have cemented a playoff berth for the first time in three years.

The Toronto Maple Leafs had hoped that 1971-72 would be their rebuilding year, but instead it turned out to be a near nightmare when crack young goalie Bernie Parent jumped to the World Hockey Association and Rick Ley, Jim Harrison and Brad Selwood followed. Coach Johnny McLellan, who had once appeared so strong behind the bench, was weakened by a nervous stomach and there was front office dissension at Maple Leaf Gardens to boot. These factors congealed to make 1972-73 a terribly uncertain season for the Maple Leafs and one that could easily find them out of the playoffs next spring.

Buffalo and Vancouver, the East Division's three-year-olds, have flourished financially but have egregiously suffered artistically since they were admitted to the NHL. The Sabres' solace has been their one-two French-Canadian scoring punch of Gil Perreault and Richard Martin, each of whom has been terribly negligent defensively. Buffalo's backline has been among the worst the NHL has known and its offense, apart from Martin, Perreault, and Gerry Meehan, rarely instills fear in the hearts of enemy goaltenders.

Vancouver is even less of a bargain. New coach Vic Stasiuk will find the cupboard even more bare than it was in his previous NHL stops—Philadelphia and Oakland—and will not be helped by his foes. Canucks captain Orland Kurtenbach is slowing down to a stop and cannot be expected to lead the team in scoring as he did last season; and after Kurtenbach there is virtually no firepower. Sophomore defenseman Josh Guevremont was third high scorer on the team in 1971-72 and, at the rate Vancouver attacks, he could be number one this year.

For the first time since Chicago was transferred to the West Division, the Black Hawks appear weakened enough to expect an authentic challenge to their rule this season. Oddly enough, it is not likely to come from the Minnesota North Stars, who finished second last year, but rather the young legs of the St. Louis Blues.

Led by Garry Unger, Jack Egers, Mike Murphy, Phil Roberto, and Barclay Plager, the Blues appear ready to leap over the North Stars, much as they did in the playoffs last spring, and give Chicago the big challenge West Division fans have awaited. The key will be the Blues' ability to come up with first-rate goaltending and the expected decline of aging Black Hawks aces and loss of Bobby Hull.

Minnesota's hopes are riding on too many senior citizens to expect anything more than third place for the North Stars, while the California Golden Seals could capture fourth if they extract special scoring from young forwards Reg Leach and Ivan Boldirev. After that the West figures to have its usual scramble between Philadelphia, led by tenacious Bobby Clarke, Pittsburgh, with crack scorer Greg Polis, and Los Angeles, featuring Juha Widing and little else. As usual injuries will be more decisive than any other factor among the mediocre expansion clubs but the guess is that once again Los Angeles will finish out of the playoffs and Red Kelly's Penguins will beat out the Flyers once more for fourth.

Which brings us to the new expansion teams, Atlanta and Long Island.

The National Hockey League draft, held in Montreal last June, had special interest for the current season because it helped stock the new teams in Atlanta and New York (Long Island). Thanks to the NHL "system", which allows the stronger clubs to retain their nucleus of stars, neither the Flames of Atlanta nor the Islanders of New York obtained a significant number of experienced personnel.

Atlanta, coached by Hall of Famer Bernie "Boom Boom" Geoffrion, collected former Canadiens goalie Phil Myre and Dan Bouchard, a netminder from the Bruins organization, giving the Flames a fair one-two combination in goal. Atlanta's better picks included Ron Harris from Detroit, Keith McCreary from Pittsburgh and Norm Gratton, a gifted forward from the Rangers' farm system.

The Islanders selected former Bruins utility ace Ed Westfall as its prime forward candidate. After swinging a deal with Montreal, Islander manager Bill Torrey came up with two experienced goaltenders, Gerry Desjardins, who had played for Los Angeles and Chicago, and Denis DeJordy, who also played for those clubs, as well as the Canadiens.

Neither of the new expansion clubs can boast anything more than enthusiasm. "We've got a young team," said

Myre, "all guys who want a chance to prove themselves . . . all players who will work hard. Not like many old guys who would just be there to collect money."

More important to the new clubs are the graduating junior players, imported from Canada's best teenage leagues. The Islanders obtained the plum, getting first choice and selecting Billy Harris, a husky right wing who had skated for the Toronto Marlboros of the Ontario Hockey Association's Junior A League. Atlanta followed with the galvanic Jacques Richard who was imported from the Quebec Remparts.

If nothing else, the youngsters will become the highest-priced rookies in hockey history, thanks to the price competition brought on by the rival World Hockey Association. "It's all a matter of money," said Harris, whose attitude was in marked contrast to the spirit of Gordie Howe and Rocket Richard, Hall of Famers who thought of playing first and money last.

When the dust of the draft meetings had cleared it appeared that the Stanley Cup-champion Bruins had been hurt most with the loss of Westfall and the defection of forward John McKenzie to the WHA's Philadelphia Blazers as player-coach.

The Montreal Canadiens, who through deals had acquired the draft picks of Los Angeles (Steve Shutt), California (Michel Larocque) and Pittsburgh (Dave Gardner) as well as its own (John Van Boxmeer) appeared to emerge the strongest along with the New York Rangers, who lost defenseman Jim Dorey to the New England Whalers.

The infant World Hockey Association will make its debut this season and already has revolutionized the face of hockey. It started by signing Bernie Parent, formerly with Toronto, for the Philadelphia Blazers and gradually other name skaters. The Alberta Oilers signed Jim Harrison, another ex-Maple Leaf. Los Angeles took former Vancouver goalie George Gardner, New England (Boston) inked Larry Pleau, who had played for Montreal, and the New York Raiders obtained Mike Robitaille who previously had skated for Buffalo, among other WHA raids.

On June 27th, 1972 the WHA dropped its biggest bombshell when Bobby Hull, the Golden Jet of the Chicago Black Hawks, put his signature on WHA contracts that supposedly will net him close to $3,000,000 over the next five years. Hull's major function was to be player-coach of the Winnipeg Jets but the NHL immediately counter-attacked, asserting that it would sue to keep Hull from playing in 1972-73 on the grounds that he was obliged to play for the Black Hawks, not the WHA Jets.

Just what effect the WHA would have on the future of professional hockey remained a moot question. Some observers predicted a quick demise of the new circuit; others insisted that it would, in time, thrive just as the NHL has flourished. One thing is certain, the WHA suddenly has made hockey a very desirable profession for a young man. "It is," said Al Eagleson, director of the NHL Players Association, "the greatest thing ever for the hockey player!"

SYL APPS, JR. The name Syl Apps has been to Canadian sports fans what Joe DiMaggio and Babe Ruth have been to American spectators. Captain and premier center of the Toronto Maple Leafs both before and after World War II, Apps led the Leafs to Stanley Cup triumphs in 1942 and then a three-straight collection from 1947 through 1949.

He scored a total of 201 goals in an era when a 200-goal career total was considered memorable and today Syl Apps, appropriately, is in the Hockey Hall of Fame.

One can easily understand, then, the immense pressures that have encumbered Syl Apps, Jr., the 25-year-old Pittsburgh Penguins center, who not only carries his dad's immortal name and plays the same position but also skates in the same lyrical style and does his job in a workmanlike and clean manner.

A university student—he attended Princeton and Queen's in Kingston, Ontario—Syl, Jr., believes the fuss over his name has abated now that he is proving himself in the National Hockey League.

"I used to feel pressures when I was growing up," said the tall, handsome Toronto native. "From kids' hockey right through my upper Junior days the fans would say that the only reason I was playing was because of my father's name. But you reach a point where, if you're not good enough, a name isn't going to win you a job. You have to do it on your own ability."

Syl, Jr., climbed from the Junior ranks to the Kingston Frontenacs Senior club and then to the New York Rangers' farm system. He played two games for Buffalo in the American League during 1968-69, scored one goal and two assists and promptly was given a "watch-carefully" tag by the New York scouts.

A season later he was transferred to Omaha of the Central Pro League and scored 16 goals and 38 assists for 54 points in 68 games. One scouting report described him thus: "Apps, Jr. is a splendid skater, a good puck-handler and playmaker, just like his father."

During the 1970 CHL playoffs he scored a league-leading ten goals and nine assists for 19 points in 12 games. He also played seven playoff games for Buffalo and managed a commendable two goals and three assists.

Always in the background was the awareness of his father's eminence in Canadian life. Syl, Sr., had become a member of the Ontario Legislature for Kingston and a member of the Cabinet.

"My father never pushed me in hockey," said Syl. "The only place he pushed me was in school. He always threatened to make me quit hockey if my marks slipped below 70. But I never did find out if he ever meant it."

The Rangers meant it when they promoted him to the big team in 1969-70; at least Syl, Jr., thought so. He started the season with New York but saw only occasional ice time and became more and more discouraged to the point of telling teammate Brad Park he wanted to quit hockey.

Syl, Jr., remembered: "At the time, the Rangers were fighting for first place and they didn't have much confidence in me. In that situation even one goal could make a difference and it was tough for them to use an inexperienced man."

On January 26, 1971, Rangers manager-coach Emile Francis solved the problem by dealing Apps to Pittsburgh for utility forward Glen Sather. Immediately Syl, Jr., became a hit in the Penguins jersey, scoring once and setting up another goal in a 3-1 win over Toronto.

"That," said Pittsburgh manager-coach Red Kelly, "was the best trade I ever made even though it was my first one. Syl really impresses me. In fact, he's got moves that even Red Berenson doesn't have."

In 31 games for Pittsburgh in 1970-71, Syl collected nine goals and 16 assists for 25 points. Last season, he led the Penguins in scoring with 15 goals and 44 assists for 59 points. It wasn't All-Star material but it impressed his father enough to win a rave.

"He just didn't get enough ice time in New York," said Poppa Apps. "I was pleased when he was traded to Pittsburgh because Red Kelly, in my estimation, is one of the outstanding NHL coaches and Syl is playing a lot of hockey."

Kelly was delighted with the results in 1971-72 and hopes for even better this season. "Syl doesn't skate as fast as his dad. Busting out of his own end, he could really hunch his shoulders and go. But I think maybe he handles the puck a bit better. Physically, he's just as strong."

Better credentials would be hard to find.

RED BERENSON There was a time not very long ago when the Detroit Red Wings dominated the hockey world the way the New York Yankees once dominated baseball. Gordie Howe was to the Red Wings what Joe DiMaggio was to the Yankees. Not far behind was the Detroit "Murderer's Row" comprising Ted Lindsay, Sid Abel, Red Kelly, and Terry Sawchuk, to name a few.

"If a hockey team went into Detroit Olympia," said Hall of Famer Frank Boucher who coached the Rangers, "and came out with a tie it was a great event in those days."

Cheers were the order of the day at the ancient arena on the corner of Grand River and McGraw. If a boo ever was heard it likely was because Pete Cusimano, the notorious octopus-tosser, had just hurled a collection of tentacles—live!—at an errant referee. And missed!

Those were the good old days in Detroit hockey. Since then there have been boos, and more boos. On the night of October 31, 1971, there were so many catcalls that coach Doug Barkley walked into manager Ned Harkness's office and handed in his resignation.

"I couldn't live with the pressure of 15,000 fans booing," said the red-faced Barkley. "And the pressure from the press, television, and radio was too much."

It was in this atmosphere that a steely-eyed, 32-year-old redhead was being asked to lead the Red Wings back to daylight, if not back to the glory days of Howe, Lindsay, and Abel. Gordon "Red" Berenson, the man in question, the center-ice refugee of the Canadiens, Rangers, and St. Louis Blues, somehow was being called upon to accomplish this impossible task.

Impossible, of course, is a big word. But what else could one say for the demands being made of Berenson, who had come to Detroit in the controversial trade in February 1971 that sent Garry Unger to St. Louis? It was a strange deal because Unger, at 23, was eight years younger than Berenson. But Harkness made the trade because he betrayed a special confidence in Red.

"We think," said Harkness, "that Berenson has the leadership qualities we want."

At the time, Gordie Howe was still skating for Detroit and was the titular leader of the club. Berenson was important, but not *that* important.

Then it happened. Howe, the greatest hockey player of all time, retired before the 1971-72 season was to begin, and suddenly the burden of leading the beleaguered Red Wings fell on the shoulders of 6-0, 190-pound Berenson.

No other player in the National Hockey League was on a hotter spot for not only was Berenson being asked to step into the immortal Howe's shoes, he was being called upon to direct a patchwork club that seemed on a treadmill to oblivion. What's more, Berenson was president of the NHL Players' Association and as such had been the center of controversy.

"Red," insists Harkness, "is a real superstar."

That just made the seat a bit hotter; and the Fahrenheit was raised still further when Berenson came to Detroit and read a headline on page one of the Detroit *News* sports section: *"UNGER TRADE 'BAD DEAL' FOR WINGS".* In plain words it was saying, Red Berenson, please go back to St. Louis. Red replied by scoring five goals and 12 assists for the Red Wings in 24 games at the tail end of the 1970-71 season. Tim Ecclestone, who accompanied Berenson to Detroit from St. Louis, was his linemate and neither displayed the brand of fervor that excites coaches. But 1970-71 was considered a lost year and 1971-72 was going to be Red's year of decision.

Coach Barkley placed him on a line with Ecclestone and Ab McDonald and Berenson failed. The Red Wings immediately described a nosedive and, without Howe, appeared on their way to a plummet through the bottom of the NHL's East Division. While Red was leading the Red Wings in scoring, his points total was hardly worth raving about—five goals in his first 15 games—and when Barkley finally resigned he obliquely indicted Berenson for letting him down. According to Harkness, Berenson was to be the leader of the club. According to Barkley the Redhead had failed.

"There's nobody leading the club," said Barkley. "The club needs a fiery leader. Berenson is not a fiery leader. He's the kind of leader Gordie Howe was. He led by example."

The difference, of course, is that Howe usually was leading the league in scoring or challenging for the top. Berenson was buried in 17th position and slipping fast. The question on the minds of Detroit hockey fans was whether Red could right himself and, hopefully, right the Red Wings. He did. Under new coach Johnny Wilson the Wings flew again and Berenson finished the 1971-72 season with an admirable record of 28 goals and 41 assists for 69 points.

Berenson himself has tried desperately to put on a happy face as if to show the hot seat hasn't been all that warm. He allowed that his first month with the Red Wings was a disaster in 1971 but 1971-72 was a whole new scene.

"There was something different about the team in 1971-72," he insisted. "It was our attitude. The problem two years ago was that we weren't happy and we had a poor attitude because of the trouble in the front office. It reflected down on all of us."

The University of Michigan All-American allowed that 1970-71 was the nadir of his NHL career, except for an earlier bench-riding stint with the Rangers. Coming off his hero-days in St. Louis, Detroit was like moving from Park Avenue to the slums.

"The problems in Detroit were understandable," he explained. "The team was playing poorly and I was playing poorly. I had a nothing reaction from the people in Olympia. I didn't deserve anything else. It was better last season. We had a lot of good young players. And it should be even better this year."

YVAN COURNOYER It was like a man knocking off ducks in a shooting gallery with a B-B gun. Except this was on ice at The Forum in Montreal and instead of a gun the man was using a hockey stick.

The shooter was a stubby little skater named Yvan Cournoyer. He plays right wing for the Montreal Canadiens and on this night in the 1969 Stanley Cup finals he was aiming at the net behind St. Louis Blues goalie Glenn Hall.

Cournoyer's stick cracked against the puck. Down, writhing in pain, went St. Louis defenseman Al Arbour as if struck by a bullet. The puck slid back to the 5-7, 169-pound French-Canadian and Cournoyer's stick blurred again.

Smack! This time Arbour's partner, Barclay Plager, topples over and the St. Louis defense lies decimated on the ice. Now 30-year-old blue-eyed Cournoyer has the puck again. Hall is at his mercy and Yvan chops the puck into the corner of the net before the All-Star goalie can make a move.

It was vintage Cournoyer, good enough to make a victim like St. Louis Vice President Lynn Patrick admit this was one of the best. "The best goal-scorer on the powerplay I've ever seen," says Patrick, "was Camille Henry. But now I have to say that this little Cournoyer is just as good."

Which helps explain why Yvan scored a hefty 47 goals and 36 assists for 83 points last season. His goal total was tops on the Canadiens.

That was no fluke. In 1970-71 Cournoyer totaled 37 goals and 36 assists for 73 points. Yvan's arsenal combines a roadrunner speed, excellent maneuverability, and, most of all, a slap shot that has a velocity above and beyond the call of Cournoyer's smallish physique.

"His shot," says goalie Joe Daley, "is right up there with

Bobby Hull's. The thing about Yvan that worries me is that he can put the puck all over—high, low, you name it—and with terrific accuracy."

Cournoyer's accuracy hit a peak in the 1968-69 season when he led the Canadiens in scoring with 43 goals and 44 assists for 87 points, sixth highest in the league. The Flying Frenchmen finished first in the East Division of the National Hockey League and went on to win the Stanley Cup. Somehow Yvan managed to play in all 76 regular season and 14 consecutive playoff contests, which is something like surviving trench warfare on the Western Front from 1914 through 1918.

Just how much longer Cournoyer can survive in the NHL jungle is questionable. "If he can manage to take the abuse without cracking," says one veteran Canadiens-watcher, "then he could be a 50-goal man like Phil Esposito or Rocket Richard."

The Rocket, of course, is Maurice Richard, the greatest of Canadiens scorers and the unofficial patron saint of Montreal hockey. "Yvan's not too big for a hockey player," say The Rocket, "but he shoots on net all the time and he's very fast."

But Richard had something that Cournoyer will never have—a powerful, almost indestructible physique and cobra-like temper that often intimidated his tormentors. Yvan is almost kittenish by comparison, and therein lies his problem. Too often for his own, or the Canadiens', good he has been tormented by the league bullies.

There was, for example, that Sunday night in Boston on December 22, 1968, when Glen Sather, then with the Bruins, took several liberties with the rule book, and Cournoyer. When the game was over Sather delivered a rather unusual—for hockey players—and candid put-down of Yvan and the other smaller Canadiens.

"You can intimidate those guys," said Sather. "I talk to them all the time. Cournoyer, all of them. I tell them they better not turn their backs on me. Things like that."

It was significant that Sather isolated Cournoyer among all the Montrealers for criticism because he singled him out for punishment again in the opening game of the Boston-Montreal East Division Stanley Cup semifinal in April 1969. Yvan, who suffered from nausea before the opening face-off, was attacked by Sather before the game was two minutes old. The Bruin bloodied Cournoyer's nose and sent Yvan to the infirmary for the rest of the period.

"Many times," Yvan admits, "I wish I was bigger because there are some guys I'd like to lick."

Whether by coincidence or not, Cournoyer was never a scoring threat in the Bruin series after his bout with Sather. Eventually coach Claude Ruel replaced him with veteran Claude Provost who embarrassed both Cournoyer and the Bruins by scoring two key goals in the fifth game of the series and who delivered the series-winning pass to captain Jean Beliveau in the sixth game.

Cournoyer is not naive enough to believe such episodes as the Sather assaults were accidents nor does he believe, as some observers do, that the bullies can really intimidate him into a bad game.

"All they do," says the scorer with a passion for fast sports cars and flashy clothes, "is get me mad. And when they get me mad I play harder. Sure, they might take care of me in a fight. I'm used to that. It really doesn't hurt my game. No, I don't care too much about it."

The one thing Yvan has cared about since he was a kid growing up in the French-speaking town of Drummondville, Quebec, has been goals. When Cournoyer was 14 his family moved to Montreal and he quickly climbed hockey's sandlot ladder. Eventually he made it to Lachine, a powerful team in the Canadiens-sponsored Metropolitain Junior League.

NHL scouts had heard good things about the slick-haired kid with the big part in his hair but they really took notice after the final game of the Lachine-Verdun series. Yvan's club was trailing by one goal with less than a minute remaining in the deciding game when he captured the puck behind his own net. Bobbing and weaving, he skated past the opposition and shot the puck past the Verdun goalie. Then he scored the winning goal in sudden-death overtime.

Eventually Cournoyer graduated to the Junior Canadiens, a teen-aged but regal version of the parent club.

This was very fortunate for the Canadiens, who were scanning the junior hockey horizon for an eventual heir apparent to Henri Richard and Jean Beliveau, the reigning French-Canadian scoring titans. The *Habitants* called him up for a five-game tryout in the 1963-64 season and he scored in his very first game. "He pounces on the puck like a cat," said former Canadiens captain Jean Beliveau.

Likening Yvan to a cat has an almost religious significance in Montreal. In all Canadiens history there was only one player who earned the nickname. That was Johnny "Black Cat" Gagnon, who twice led the team in scoring six and seven years before Cournoyer was born. Like Yvan, Gagnon was a right winger. Soon they were calling Yvan "The Black Cat II."

Former Montreal coach Toe Blake was less enthused about Cournoyer than the phrase-makers. He gave Yvan only part-time work during his rookie year, 1964-65, and Cournoyer scored only seven goals. "But I never let down," says Yvan, "because when you let down you're finished. I said to myself eventually I would have my chance."

A season later he had scored 18 goals but still was used almost exclusively on the power play. By 1966-67 he was up to 25 goals but Blake remained critical of Yvan's defensive play. Then the coach decided to gamble and use him as a regular right wing and, amazingly, Cournoyer's defensive record immediately improved. "Toe kept harping at it," says Yvan, "and I kept working at it."

It was just as well that Blake put him on a line with Beliveau and hard-rock John Ferguson because the French-speaking clientele at The Forum had become impatient with the coach.

"On veut Cournoyer" (we want Cournoyer) was a standard chant when Yvan wasn't on the ice and the demands increased as his goal total climbed. He reached 28 in 1967-68 and on March 12, 1969, he scored his fortieth goal of the 1968-69 season. With eight games left in the schedule it was almost possible for Yvan to reach the 50-goal plateau. But he only scored three more and actually felt relieved about the whole thing.

"If I decided that I had to score fifty," he says, "everytime I missed a goal I should have scored I'd have brooded over it. That's no good. If you keep brooding you stop getting your chances."

One of Cournoyer's major assets—his skating speed—has also been responsible for his failure to score 50 goals. In the 1968 Stanley Cup quarter-final against Boston, for example, he missed four breakaways because he was moving too fast for his own good.

"I've had problems with goals I didn't get on breakaways," he admits. "But I have a theory about breakaways —the more time you have to think about what you're going to do the more things there are to think about. So you make a mistake."

The biggest mistake Yvan made in 1969-70 was getting in front of a flying puck on Saturday night, October 25, 1969, at The Forum. The puck broke his nose and sidelined him for two weeks.

Montreal's general manager Sam Pollock considers Yvan the man who must fuel the Canadiens' scoring machine in the post-Jean Beliveau years now that the distinguished captain has retired. It is a problem that has not exactly eluded Yvan.

"If the players want a guy and look up to him he is the leader," Cournoyer explains. "I don't know if that would happen to me or if we'd all want somebody else."

There is an element of doubt in his voice, and with good reason. "When they talk about Cournoyer being a successor to Beliveau," says Toronto goalie Jacques Plante, "they're basing it all on Yvan's scoring, which isn't all there is to leadership. There's a big gap between a great scorer and a team leader."

Others argue that Yvan is still learning and improving and is not likely to take a backward step. Certainly Yvan has a quiet confidence that surfaces in odd ways. There was the night early in the 1967-68 season after he had scored his sixth goal in his sixth game.

He was leaning back against the dressing room wall when teammate Henri Richard walked over with a bottle of soda. Yvan picked up one of his skates, pressed the head of the bottle against the blade and flipped off the cap. "Keep doing that," warned trainer Larry Aubut, "and it'll hurt your skating."

Cournoyer stared back at Aubut. "It hasn't yet and I'm not going to start doing anything different now." Which is quite alright with Sam Pollock and the Canadiens' front office.

KEN DRYDEN The most marketable commodity in professional hockey is neither Bobby Orr, Derek Sanderson, Brad Park, or Bobby Hull. It is 25-year-old Ken Dryden—scholar, orator, lawyer-to-be, and goaltender for the Montreal Canadiens.

Dryden who stands 6-3½ and weighs 210 pounds, means more things to more people than any of the top-drawer stickhandlers and his star shines brighter with every game and personal appearance.

Unlike Orr, who never graduated from high school, Dryden has a B.A. from Cornell University and has a mortgage on a law degree from McGill University.

Unlike Sanderson, swing-man of the ice, Dryden is cool without being offensive.

Unlike Park, who is buried in the non-hockey atmosphere of Manhattan, Dryden reigns as prince valiant in the puck monarchy that is Montreal.

Unlike Hull, an aging glamor boy trying to make it in the WHA, Dryden is dashing, and could be mistaken for a Hollywood star if Hollywood was still producing stars of the Errol Flynn genre.

What makes the Dryden day-to-day saga so remarkable is that while some of his NHL colleagues spend their waking hours trying to determine which movie to see, he was occupied for two seasons with a full-time law school schedule while playing full-time for the Canadiens.

"It was more difficult in my first year than it was in the second season," said Dryden. "Two seasons ago I had required courses which were given early in the morning, when we had practice.

"In the second season I took elective courses and most of them were later in the afternoon. My hockey day, when we didn't have a game, was finished at noon. The only difficult time was when exams came around—I didn't have as much time as I should to prepare for them."

But the inevitable conflict developed during Christmas 1971.

"We had a Western trip," Ken recalled, "that went from Sunday to Sunday, and I had exams just prior to the first Sunday, and one on the Tuesday after we came back. We also played Toronto that Wednesday, making it a bit difficult."

If an exam was given when Dryden was on the road he would forfeit the exam and take the consequent punishment rather than abandon the Canadiens.

"I'd have had no choice," he explained. "I am a full-time hockey player and I'm required to be at all games, practices, team functions, and everything else. What the Law School would probably do is have me take the exam at the same time wherever I was. For example, if I was in Los Angeles I'd take the exam at six in the morning if the exam was scheduled for nine in the morning back in Montreal, and it would be monitored by someone chosen by the University."

It has been suggested from time to time that Dryden eventually will quit the NHL and concentrate on more scholarly pursuits. Recently, however, he has indicated that he enjoys hockey so much he might try to do both. "I'll probably end up practicing law in Canada," he said.

Dryden never experienced nearly the intense mental fatigue in his dual role that others do just thinking about his full-time playing and full-time studying. As a matter of fact, he believes school helped his hockey and vice versa.

"It's a definite advantage to have some other interests besides hockey," said Dryden. "On the other hand it's also an advantage to have something besides studies. I think I'd have had a very difficult time spending long hours in the library without looking forward to hockey practice.

"At Cornell University, for example, I used to play my worst games over Christmas vacation when I had nothing else to do. When you're involved in several things you sort of keep going—almost on nervous energy at times."

Almost from the start of last season Montreal coach Scotty Bowman insisted that Dryden was the woof and warp of the Canadiens. Nobody paid much attention to Bowman until Ken was sidelined with a back injury and the Flying Frenchmen looked like creeping turtles.

"We were floundering," Ken admitted while ineffectually trying to deflect praise from himself. "But there's really no one key to the reason why. It was just the way we played against the teams that weren't challenging us. We didn't play well against those teams. I think we got too tight for those games, for fear of losing. We'd win big if we just went out and tried to enjoy ourselves but we act just the opposite. Even when we'd win it would be something like 3-2 when it should have been 8-2."

A former member of Canada's National Hockey Team, Ken has a much more comprehensive knowledge of international hockey than his NHL compatriots. He knows just how good the Russian stickhandlers are and believes that they could adapt to NHL hockey without any trouble. He shares that opinion about the Czechs.

What's more, Dryden appreciates the international approach to hockey rather than the philistine ideas of many NHL types.

"The Russians and Czechs approach hockey a lot differently," Dryden said. "Their whole method of coaching and instruction is superior to ours. I, for one, never learned anything from a coach. But over there, the best goalies publish an instructional booklet which is available to young goaltenders all over the country, which has to be a tremendous improvement.

"I think they'd look at an NHL game very logically. For example, why does Dave Keon forecheck as well as he does? What is he actually doing? I think we have a tendency to play it sort of haphazardly. I think the reason the NHL doesn't take a logical incisive look at its games is that there are so many games, that practices are used as a rest period, rather than a time to analyze the opposition."

Dryden believes the current NHL schedule is "too long" but allows that it may be necessary so that teams can pay higher salaries. As for himself, he's content to play 60 to 65 games but couldn't see himself going through an entire season without taking a rest.

"The pressure of knowing that you had to play every game for the next few months would really be something," he said. "For me it would have been unbearable to play when there was the one-goalie system."

First and foremost on Dryden's agenda is helping regain the Stanley Cup for the Canadiens. When Ken was awarded the Calder Trophy last spring as rookie of the year, he

made it clear that that was *not* the prize he really wanted.
"I would have much rather turned in my Calder Trophy,"
said Dryden, "for the Stanley Cup. Winning the Calder
was meaningful to me but there's only *ONE* real trophy to
win and that's the Cup."

Dryden also was runner-up in the 1972 voting for the
Hart Trophy as the NHL's most valuable player. He
polled 89 votes to the 126 collected by Boston's Bobby
Orr. "I was surprised I did that well in the Hart voting,"
said Dryden.

But Canadiens manager Sam Pollock expected it. After
all, Dryden played in 64 regular season games during the
1971-72 season, more than any other goaltender, and
produced an impressive 2.24 goals against average.

Winning the rookie award was rather unusual since
Dryden had played six regular season games and 20
playoff games in 1970-71. But NHL rules stipulate that a
rookie is a "rookie" if he has played in fewer than 25
regular season games so Ken qualified for the prize in
1971-72 and beat out Richard Martin of Buffalo and
Marcel Dionne of Detroit. Dryden said he wasn't overly
surprised at winning the award.

"I thought the biggest thing might be the feeling that I
wasn't really a rookie," he said. "Given that and the fact
that Dionne and Martin had such very good seasons I
didn't know what to expect."

But that's the story of Dryden's life. Between law
school, goaltending, and consumer affairs, one just doesn't
know what to expect from him next.

PHIL ESPOSITO It is a measure of Phil Esposito's ac-
complishments as an offensive ace that his style of
"camping in the slot" was copied by New York Rangers
left wing Vic Hadfield last season and Hadfield scored 50
goals.

As remarkable as Hadfield's mark might have been—

he was the first Ranger to reach 50—it paled in comparison to Esposito's mathematics. Playing in 76 games, Phil scored 66 goals and 67 assists for a league-leading total of 133 points, 16 more than runner-up Bobby Orr.

Combined with Bobby Orr, Esposito gave the Boston Bruins a one-two punch that enabled them to win the Stanley Cup and terrorize National Hockey League goaltenders from Vancouver to Montreal.

"Esposito and Orr run the Bruins' offense," said Bobby Hull of the Chicago Black Hawks. "Orr creates the situation and Esposito puts it away. They work perfectly together. They know that when one of them has the puck something is going to happen."

In addition Phil has been significantly helped by his big wingers Ken Hodge and Wayne Cashman, who control the boards and neutralize anyone who may disturb their center. Of course, disturbing Esposito is not all that easy. At 6-1, 210 pounds, he generally camps about 20 feet in front of the enemy goal as if he's a permanent monument.

"Esposito is big and strong and hard to move," said New York Rangers general manager-coach Emile Francis. "But you can't let him camp out there in the slot and wait for passes. He's too dangerous. He can hurt you too much."

With that in mind, Francis assigned his hard-nosed center Walt Tkaczuk the job of guarding Esposito during the 1972 Stanley Cup finals. The results were surprisingly gratifying for Francis and distressing for Esposito. In six games Esposito didn't score a single goal.

"Tkaczuk," said Esposito, "had a job to do and he did it well. But the Ranger defensemen gave me cross-checks, pitch-forks, hooks and the works. I felt like I was in a brawl and lost."

If Esposito lost anything it was the respect of Madison Square Garden fans for his persistent complaints to referees and general irritability over the treatment meted out by the Rangers. There were those who contend that Tkaczuk has begun to overtake Esposito as the NHL's leading center and will do so in a season or two. "If I had a choice," said St. Louis Blues broadcaster Gus Kyle, "I'd go with Tkaczuk."

Of course, Esposito has his boosters, even when he doesn't score. Bruins coach Tom Johnson pointed out last spring that Phil didn't necessarily have to score to help

Boston to the Stanley Cup. "A lot of people overlooked Espie's major contribution," said Johnson, "which was winning face-offs."

Still there is widespread belief that the Bruins could win without Esposito but not without Orr. And that Phil's records are as flimsy as the paper on which they are printed. A sign hanging in Madison Square Garden one night said it all:

"Esposito, A Product of Inflationary NHL Expansion."

The point was quite obvious. If not for the California Golden Seals, Los Angeles Kings, and Vancouver Canucks, Esposito hardly would have been able to break the scoring records made by Maurice "Rocket" Richard and Gordie Howe.

The point was underlined during the 1971 Stanley Cup playoffs when Esposito was confronted with the Montreal Canadiens in a seven-game series. He performed like a mediocre skater.

Needless to say, Esposito refuses to believe his critics. He blasted the anti-Phil claque during an interview with *Newsweek* sports editor Pete Axthelm.

"They talk about how the game has slipped," Esposito complained to Axthelm; "they talk about Richard's 50 goals in only 50 games; but they don't mention that it happened in a war year—when the talent was as diluted as it's ever been."

Nobody can question Phil as the best center in hockey. His credentials include election to the NHL's First All-Star Team and the Art Ross Trophy for the past two seasons.

Esposito has favorable points to make. "The game to-day," said Phil, "is twice as fast as it was in the old days. The players shoot twice as often and twice as hard."

"Phil," said Bruins chief scout Red Sullivan, "is one of the great all-time players in front of the net. He has the moves. He always comes up with the puck."

Playing on a line with rugged Cashman and equally opponents in the corners and fetch him the puck for the bullish Hodge, Esposito relies on his wings to outrough *coup de grace.*

"We didn't set records because of weak opponents," said Phil. "We did it because of our overall offensive philosophy. We hit, we get position in front of the net, we shoot, we help each other ... You know what I really think about all the comparison between our records and the older ones? I think there's never been a hockey club that could tie our skates."

That particular point was thrown in Esposito's face in the spring of 1971 by the triumphant Canadiens. After his team had been wiped out in the seventh and final game at Boston Garden, Esposito accepted part of the blame. A reporter had asked him if he had been frustrated.

"I don't know," he replied. "Disappointed, maybe ... let down, maybe ... kind of angry at myself ... my team ... the Canadiens deserved to win ... we didn't."

Esposito's regular season performance in 1971-72 emphasized his consistency to critics and impressed opponents with its diversity. "He's forever trying new shooting tricks," said Toronto goalie Jacques Plante. "There's no single shot you can watch for from him. Phil makes a point of remembering the habits and weaknesses of players on the other teams, especially the goalies, and he plays to their weaknesses, not their strengths."

The question remains whether opponents will pick up where Walt Tkaczuk left off last spring and continue to try to exploit Phil Esposito's weakness: his irritability with being closely checked. It could go a long way in determining just how bright a superstar he really is.

PAUL HENDERSON It was snowing one of those old-fashioned Ontario snows that today's Toronto people call a blizzard. The time was January 28, 1943—6 a.m. The place, a country road somewhere between Amberley and Kincardine in Bruce County.

A sleigh plowing through the flakes gave it a Currier and Ives aura, except for one thing: a baby was being born in the sleigh to Mr. and Mrs. Garnet Henderson. Before the sleigh ever reached Kincardine Hospital a wailing Paul Henderson made his first appearance on ice.

To say the least Henderson's debut was curious then and even stranger considered in retrospect. As a professional hockey player first with the Detroit Red Wings and then with the Toronto Maple Leafs, Henderson betrayed a bizarre ailment known as trachitis. He gagged and coughed when cold air hit his lungs, especially on National Hockey League rinks.

In time it was cured and lucky for the NHL cash registers, too, because the speedy helmeted left wing now completing his eighth big-league season has emerged as one of the most exciting scorers of the seventies. Not to mention the No. 1 holler guy on the Leafs.

"That's why Paul gets so many breakaways," says veteran goalie Jacques Plante. "He yells for the puck. When he gets a break between two defensemen he'll shout for the puck and his linesmen will throw it to him."

It worked to the tune of 30 goals and 30 assists in the 1970-71 season and was even better last year. In fact, Henderson scored a personal high of 38 goals and was a major reason why Toronto was a factor in the East Division race.

Henderson's value to the Toronto sextet was obvious from the opening game of the season last October 8 in Vancouver. Paul was all over the ice and scored the tying goal in what eventually was a 3-2 Leaf win. It was so rare a performance that losing coach Hal Laycoe couldn't find time to blast his own club.

"Henderson was sensational," Laycoe said. "In the final analysis his performance made the difference."

Typically, Paul was less than enthused. He had scored one goal but he wanted five. That's not so much a function of greed as it is the fact that he usually misses more than he gets because of his break-the-sound-barrier speed. It's an old NHL bromide that Henderson is too fast for his own good.

"Henderson would be high man on the totem pole," said Toronto *Daily Star* columnist Milt Dunnell, "if they kept figures on the number of breakaways that misfire."

"Last season," Henderson said, "I could think of 30 breakaways and I think I scored twice."

One night at Maple Leaf Gardens in a game against Minnesota hard-luck Henderson had three clean breakaways and four other scoring chances at the North Stars' net but came away from the game with one assist.

"It's amazing how he gets loose so often for those clear tries on goal," said ex-Leaf George Armstrong.

Paul's ex-boss Punch Imlach added, "I've never seen a player have such rotten luck around the goal."

Actually, Henderson has suffered worse luck. Once, he watched in horror as referee Art Skov disallowed a goal he had scored against the Flyers in Philadelphia and on the following night came close to beating up the Maple Leaf Gardens' goal judge Eddie Mepham after another near-catastrophe on his home ice.

What had happened was that the Leafs and St. Louis Blues were tied, 2-2, with less than three minutes remaining in the game when Henderson flipped the puck high into the Blues net. For reasons best known to the goal judge he failed to signal the goal light. Realizing that still another goal was about to be "stolen" from him, Henderson headed for the glass at the north end of Maple Leaf Gardens in an attempt at Mepham's scalp.

"I was ready to go over the wall," Paul said. "It looked as if I was being cold-decked by a goal judge in our own building. I knew the puck was in, although a bit higher than I had intended. But I couldn't have placed it in the net any better with my own hand."

A split-second before Henderson reached the glass he noticed that the referee had signalled with arm motions that it was, in fact, a score. "If the ref hadn't signalled the goal," Henderson insisted, "I know I'd have gone over the glass."

Mostly, Paul is a temperate type, not given to outbursts, and has been a sportsman more than a slugger ever since he learned to play hockey in Kincardine.

His father, the late Garnet Henderson, coached Paul during his peewee days. When young Henderson was 11 years old he scored six goals for his club (Lucknow, Ontario) in a peewee tournament which Lucknow won, 7-2. Eventually Paul moved up the traditional hockey ladder, from peewee to juvenile leagues, and at age 15 he scored 18 goals and assisted on two others in a 21-3 win for his club. Henderson attributes those inflationary figures to the fact that he learned to shoot high faster than his peers.

An 18-goal game by a kid anywhere from Lucknow to the Yukon sends big blips on the NHL scouting radar screen and, naturally, they went looking for Henderson.

The Henderson family was turned off by the *gauche* approach of the Leafs. Boston's scout, Harold Cotton, proved more convincing until Jimmy Skinner, the Red Wings' bird dog, suggested that Henderson drop over to Hamilton, Ontario, and visit the Detroit minor camp enroute to the Boston base in Niagara Falls.

"Jimmy said I could use a few days of conditioning in Hamilton before going to Niagara Falls," Paul recalled. "As it turned out I never did leave Hamilton."

He played three years of solid Junior A hockey for the Hamilton Red Wings and added a Memorial Cup (emblematic of Canada's Junior championship) to his repertoire in 1962. By this time the Detroit Red Wings were casting expectant eyes on the 5-11, 180-pounder but Paul had his eyes on a teaching career.

The decision between pro hockey and college didn't come easy. His mother wanted him to become a teacher; his dad preferred that he take a shot at the NHL. Skinner's influence as well as the elder Henderson turned Paul in the direction of Detroit.

"I had doubts about my own ability to make it in the NHL," Paul said. "That was before expansion and I wasn't a very good stickhandler although I knew I could skate and shoot pretty well. Jimmy built up my ego. He said he thought I could make it and I had always known that if Jimmy said something his word was good."

Henderson suffered the same fate that befell other gifted Juniors who arrived in Detroit during the late fifties and early sixties. Inevitably, the word was trumpeted, "He'll be the next Gordie Howe."

In 1963-64 Henderson scored a grand total of three goals in 32 games and people began saying he will be, in fact, the next Gordie Howe. A season later he scored eight goals in 70 games and they said he'd be the next Val Fonteyne. But in 1965-66 he scored 22 goals and 24 assists for 46 points in 69 games and, as a topper, potted three goals and three assists in 12 playoff games.

On March 3, 1968, Henderson was involved in one of the bigger flesh-peddling episodes the NHL has known. He was traded to Toronto with Norm Ullman and Floyd

Smith in exchange for Frank Mahovlich, Garry Unger, and Peter Stemkowski. Significantly, Henderson and Ullman are the ones who have remained with the teams to which they then were traded.

Henderson had nothing to worry about. His scoring in Toronto was a distinct improvement over anything he did in Detroit and he scored five goals in the six playoff games last spring. It obviously was no fluke, as proven by the 1971-72 mathematics and some genuine "college try" by Henderson.

"Henderson scored 38 goals last year and I think he must have gotten most of them because of his speed," said Ken Hodge of the Boston Bruins, who sometimes has to cover the Maple Leafs' star. "You can be right with Paul, skating at what you feel is maximum speed, and then suddenly he'll shift gears and tear away from you."

Henderson replies: "Lines score goals in hockey, not individuals," Paul explained. "Without the two guys you've got with you—well, you're nothing.

"Take Ullman, for example," he continued. "A lot of times Norm will move out of his center position when we're in the attacking zone so that I can have the slot in front of the goalie. Then he'll pass me the puck where I can do something with it.

"But all the fans ever remember is that I was the guy who scored the goal. It's the same way with Ron Ellis. He digs the puck out of his corner, sets me up in front of the net, and I get all the credit."

It's rare for a man who shoots right to play left wing. Paul, however, is among a handful of NHL players who have been successful at it.

"Moving to the wrong side of the ice is quite an adjustment at first," Henderson explained.

"For me, it was maybe a happy accident, since it got me a regular job. But I wouldn't advise it for everybody. What happened is this.

"I was with Detroit when I made the change. They had me listed as a right wing, only there were so many guys ahead of me I seldom got to play. Then one of the team's left wings got hurt. They put me over there, I scored a couple of goals, an dthe first thing I knew I had a job.

"But if you're a natural right-hand shot, it's awfully hard to take the puck off the boards on your left side.

You have to stop and turn before you can pass to anyone. And it's also difficult to get any power into your backhand.

"But there is one very obvious advantage to a right hander playing the left side—the blade of your stick sees a great deal more of the goalie's cage when you shoot. In other words, it kind of gives you an extra corner to aim at."

There was the episode in December 1971 when Paul was nursing an injury in Toronto when the Leafs were in Pittsburgh preparing for a game against the Penguins. Henderson was considered inactive until he decided to grab a late plane for Pittsburgh. He arrived just before game time, suited up and set up Ullman with the insurance goal in a 4-2 Leaf win. He also managed to give Pittsburgh winger John Stewart a charley horse with a legal check in the third period.

It was the kind of effort that nearly inspired a member of the Leaf camp to sputter something about Toronto owning another Gordie Howe.

Right now they'd be content with one more Paul Henderson.

BOBBY HULL It is a commentary on our contemporary values that Bobby Hull was more renowned last season for having 90 hair transplants than for scoring his 600th National Hockey League goal.

Or that he has received more ink over a $3,000,000, five-year offer to jump to Winnipeg's World Hockey Association team than he did for scoring 50 or more goals for the fifth time in his NHL career. Bobby eventually shook the hockey world by accepting the WHA.

Or that the former Chicago Black Hawks left wing supposedly has been bumped from the top of the golden iceberg by Bobby Orr when, in fact, the Hull money machine never has meshed more smoothly.

If Hull didn't singlehandedly hoist the Hawks into a first-place finish for the third straight year, he certainly didn't hurt them. The only people hurt by his 50 goals, 43 assists, and 93 points played in cities other than the Windy one. The Golden Jet has, in fact, scored more goals than any player now in the NHL. He is something like a skating legend, or whatever they call the best in his trade.

More than that, he has been the most glamorous shinny ambassador over the past decade, patiently delivering lengthy interviews with newsmen when a Bobby Orr will hide in the trainer's room, and endlessly signing autographs when a Derek Sanderson will tell a lad to bugger-off.

"Bobby was like that wherever we played," said ex-Hawk teammate Chico Maki. "People want to be near Bobby and he obliges. And we held the bus for him."

There's nothing phony about Hull, or if there is, he has carefully managed to conceal it from the probers and his teammates.

"I've never seen him turn his back on a kid," said goalie Tony Esposito. "He considers autograph signing an obligation."

There are those who will tell you that a Hull autograph has dropped in value the way a dollar does at the height of inflation. They say that the young ones—Orr, Brad Park, Richard Martin, Garry Unger—are the men of the hour and that Hull is a couple of years away from has-been-ism.

Don't believe it.

Boston Bruins goalie Gerry Cheevers doesn't. He's still looking for the shell that exploded off Hull's stick March 25, 1972, and careened into the webbing behind him. Hull's 600th goal. Significantly, the man fumbling on his knees, futilely trying to stop Hull, was none other than Orr.

Some day, of course, Orr may score 600 goals. Hull no doubt will be a 50-year-old cattle rancher at the time and he'll accept the erasure with the same equanimity with which he approaches hockey and his new job as player coach of the Winnipeg Jets.

If Bobby ever labored with a large albatross on his back, it was in the 1971 Stanley Cup finals when Montreal's Rejean Houle (5-11, 165 pounds) shadowed every step taken by the 5-10, 195-pound Hull.

"What could I do?" said Hull. "Nothing could help unless the referee called a penalty. My name is not Samson."

Houle became a member of a long line of shadows who have haunted Bobby ever since he climbed to the superstar plateau by scoring 50 goals in 1961-62.

"Things haven't changed all these years," said Hull. "These guys are put out there for a specific job and they've got to do it or they'll get somebody else. I get a little frustrated, that's all."

Pittsburgh's Bryan Watson was the worst—when Super Pest played for Detroit—until one night Hull nearly jammed Watson's esophagus down to his heel. Ed Westfall of the Bruins had been a bother and defenseman Brad Park of New York has traded blows with Bobby.

"Hull is a fair player," said Houle, "probably more fair than me. He never gave me a really dirty check. Sometimes he'd hit me, but he had to do something."

That's the way millionaire Ben Hatskin felt when he acquired the Winnipeg WHA franchise last summer. He had to do something so he went out and signed Bobby Hull, which was like moving Chicago Stadium to the Aleutian Islands. Almost.

But Hatskin had a sense of modern history and one of the lessons he learned was that in the fall of 1969 the Chicago Black Hawks' front office publicly humiliated Bobby and he still was smarting over the episode. It happened over a contract dispute during which Hull missed training camp and the first 14 games of the regular season.

"Bobby's action cost him a lot of bad publicity and substantial financial loss," said Tony Esposito. "The club fined him $1,500 for each game he missed. So he came back because he had to. He's got many investments, many enterprises, and he needed the cash to protect these investments."

He's also got pride, and the public whipping did not enhance his affection for the people who run the Black Hawks. Then along came the WHA and Hatskin. His offer was in the neighborhood of $3,000,000 for five seasons. Bobby accepted.

While Hull sometimes may be soupy and saccharine and artificially nice, there remains a basic pleasantness about him that rarely disappears. It did once years ago in New York when he complained about a magazine article which was accompanied by an especially ugly picture of the man. His vanity got the best of him and he screamed blue epithets at the writer.

Mostly, though, he's the kind of guy who last year went on a CBS-TV network interview and refused the suggestion that Boston Garden fans are animals. Instead, Hull lauded the Bostonians for their knowledge and appreciation of hockey.

Or he's this kind of guy. Late in the 1971-72 season he had 48 goals and broke away with teammate Chris Bordeleau against St. Louis with the Blues' net empty. Bobby then waited in vain for Bordeleau's pass. It never came, but Hull never beefed.

Instead of skimming the puck to Hull, Bordeleau flipped it into the open net himself. Coach Billy Reay ripped Bordeleau for his selfish indiscretion, insisting that he should have passed off to Hull.

Hull realized that mediocre types such as Bordeleau need all the goals they can get. Bobby could have been browned off. Instead, he chuckled at the fuss and defended Bordeleau for doing his thing, putting the puck into the net.

"After all," said Bobby Hull, "he's doing a good job."

That's why Winnipeg will love the Golden Jet.

ORLAND KURTENBACH When rangy Orland Kurtenbach was drafted from the New York Rangers by Vancouver on June 10, 1970, it hardly was considered a momentous move on the part of either team. The 6-2, 195 native of Cudworth, Saskatchewan, was believed to be washed-up—a labored skater whose value to New York could be summed up in the four goals he scored in 53 games during the 1969-70 season.

But a metamorphosis took place in Kurtenbach's play

that made Vancouver, in its first NHL season, a playoff threat through Christmas week 1970. The Canucks were cruising along in fourth place, led by "Big Kurt" who had amassed 14 goals and 23 assists in 34 games. It was the first time he had ever averaged a-point-a-game in the NHL.

"I can't explain it," Kurt said at the time. "It's true that now that I'm the team captain I'm in a slightly different role. Before, I was always the third center, specializing in checking assignments. Now, I'm getting a chance to spend more time on the ice and to work on power plays. That's made a difference, simply because I'm getting more opportunities. Shots are going in for me. My passes are getting to where I want them to go. It's just the way it is in sports."

On the night of December 23, 1970, the Canucks were playing Toronto at Maple Leaf Gardens. Kurt had the puck and looked up too late to discover that he was about to be creamed.

When Kurt got to his feet he knew he was in trouble. His left knee throbbed with pain and he limped to the sidelines with what later was diagnosed as torn ligaments. When Canucks manager Bud Poile learned the extent of the injury he asserted that it was tantamount to having one's right arm amputated.

By Vancouver standards Poile was right. Kurt missed 27 games and during that spell Vancouver lost 19 matches and tied three. The club fell out of a playoff berth and never recovered its equilibrium until the captain returned, modest as always.

"It's been said often enough that I mean something to this club," said Kurt. "Personally, I can't very well not be aware of it."

Poile was aware as anyone. "It all turned around for us that first season starting with that December twenty-third game," said the Canucks manager. "We went 11 games without winning and Toronto went 14 without losing. That killed us, as far as fourth place was concerned."

When Kurt returned, too late to help, he regained his groove and managed to score a total of 21 goals and 32 assists for 53 points in 52 games.

The glory was a long time coming for Kurt, a 36-year-old who once was labelled "the million-dollar prospect" when he played junior hockey for the Prince Albert, Saskatchewan, Mintos.

For reasons best known to Orland himself, he never fulfilled the raves received as a junior. He played almost everywhere—Saskatoon, Buffalo, Springfield, Providence, San Francisco, and minor-league Vancouver—before landing a permanent job in the NHL with Boston in 1963-64.

But his scoring was weak and on June 8, 1965, Kurt was dealt to Toronto with Pat Stapleton and Andy Hebenton for Ron Stewart. He lasted only a year with the Maple Leafs before being drafted by the Rangers.

Curiously enough it was Kurtenbach who beat Red Berenson out of a center ice job with the Rangers, inspiring coach Emile Francis to deal Berenson to St. Louis.

On Broadway, Kurt had some good nights. In 1966-67 he managed 11 goals and 25 assists for 36 points in 60 games but his mathematics tailed off after that, followed by a spinal fusion operation that detoured—but saved—his career. Coming to Vancouver lengthened it indefinitely.

"We didn't necessarily think of him as a big scorer," said former Canucks coach Hal Laycoe. "We thought of him as a leader because of his competitive approach to hockey, his class as an individual and his ability to handle the rough going."

And just to prove that his leadership in 1970-71 was not a mirage, Kurtenbach recovered from his injury last season and played a full 78-game schedule. While he was at it he scored 24 goals, 37 assists for 61 points, tied for the team leadership on Vancouver.

It wasn't enough to provide the Canucks with a playoff berth, but without Kurtenbach it is hard to imagine Vancouver even surviving in the NHL.

GUY LAPOINTE It was in the first period of a game between the Montreal Canadiens and Detroit Red Wings at Olympia Stadium in November 1971. The puck skimmed out to Detroit forward Al Karlander who was stationed just outside the Canadiens' blue line. In the split-second that it took for him to wind up and crash his stick against the puck Montreal's sloe-eyed defenseman Guy Lapointe hurled his 6-0, 185-pound body in front of the flying rubber.

The puck deflected off Guy's stick blade and carommed high and hard into the Canadiens defenseman's face, less than an inch below his right eye. "It felt," says Guy, "as if I got hit by a boulder."

He crumpled to the ice while teammates wondered whether the gifted 24-year-old defenseman suddenly was at the end of his career. "When it's up there," says Montreal coach Scotty Bowman, "you always worry about the eye."

Lapointe was lucky. He was removed to the hospital with a fractured cheekbone but his sight was not impaired. A few weeks later he was back on the ice, working out with a protective face mask to guard him until the injury completely healed. This is what Lapointe is all about. "I love hockey so much," he says, "I'd play it for nothing."

The admiration is mutual between Lapointe and Bowman. "His performance," says the coach, "speaks for itself. Besides his scoring, he has one of the best defensive records." When the 1971-72 season was over Guy had compiled 11 goals, 38 assists and 49 points and was improving with every week.

Which explains why Guy managed to nudge his way into a regular spot on a team laden with such defensive artists as Terry Harper, Jacques Laperriere, Serge Savard, and Pierre Bouchard. A couple of injuries—to Savard and Laperriere—provided the opening and his efforts in the 1971 playoffs assured his future in Montreal. He played in 20 Stanley Cup games, scored four goals and nine assists for 13 points, and generally conducted himself like a seasoned pro, although Guy claims there was turbulence inside of him.

"I really was scared of making a mistake," he allows, "especially in the finals with Chicago. It was really terrible. I got sick before the game and between each period."

Perhaps part of the problem was that he still remembered that he was playing alongside his childhood heroes, particularly Laperriere. "When I was 14," Guy recalls, "my neighborhood team in Montreal won a championship and it was Jacques who gave me a trophy. I wasn't very big then and when I look at the picture of that ceremony today I still say 'Imagine that! Me playing with Jacques Laperriere.' "

Those were days when Guy had little confidence in his pro hockey future. At age 18 he planned to become a cop and enlisted in the Quebec Provincial Police. It was a perfectly natural idea since his brother had been a cop with the Montreal Police Department and his dad was a captain in the Montreal Fire Department for 25 years. But the Canadiens intervened, offering him a spot with the Junior Canadiens, and Guy accepted.

Unlike the more flamboyant Bobby Orr and Brad Park, Lapointe's defensive skills are less obtrusive but appreciated nonetheless. "He's strong," says ex-Canadiens captain Jean Beliveau. "Not just when he shoots, but in everything he does. He does everything strong."

One reason for that is the fact that he does 20 push-ups every night and again when he gets up in the morning and plays a fast game of handball regularly. Besides, he never seems to get enough hockey in to suit himself.

Of all the problems Lapointe has had in hockey the most difficult was learning to speak English while he played for the Canadiens' farm team in Houston in 1968-69. English-speaking players mocked him. "If it wasn't for Phil Myre, who was my roommate, I don't know what might have happened."

A year later he was promoted to the Montreal Voyageurs of the American League and finally up, permanently, with the Canadiens. "I'm never satisfied with my game," he insists. "That's why you'll notice me always nearly the last player to leave the ice in practice."

But one of the first to rate future consideration as an All-Star.

FRANK MAHOVLICH Who else in the NHL today has made four comebacks? Yes, count them, four comebacks, and yet who was accused of being in a "prolonged slump," simply because he didn't score his 20th goal until January 1, 1972, of the 1971-72 season?

Who else in the NHL could tie one playoff record (27 points in Stanley Cup competition, 1971, shared with Boston's Phil Esposito) and break another (14 goals, again in the 1971 playoffs), yet end up a poor third in news coverage, behind a rookie goaltender and a younger brother whose major claim to fame is mischief rather than goals?

And who else in the NHL runs a prosperous travel agency in Toronto and is seriously thinking of taking up painting?

Why, none other than Montreal's Frank Mahovlich, of course.

As a matter of fact, the Gulliverian left winger's long-time nickname, "The Big M," is more apropos of the epithet "The Big Misunderstanding" than it is of his size—six feet, 205 pounds—which originally earned him the label.

Frank's first misunderstanding and subsequent comeback took place before he even got really started in the NHL.

After a brilliant junior career at St. Michael's College (high school) in Toronto, Mahovlich was called up to the Maple Leafs during the 1956-57 season and played a mediocre three-game tryout. He scored one goal, but sophisticated Toronto fans were disappointed in the highly touted youngster.

The next season Frank "came back" to score 20 goals and win the Calder Cup as Rookie of the Year. Although it was his first NHL season, Frank tasted the criticism he was to know throughout his career. Coach Billy Reay made it publicly obvious that he had expected more than 20 goals from the prodigy.

Frank's next two seasons were competent, but less than star quality—22 goals in 1958-59 and a sorrowful 18 the following year. This wasn't bad, mind you, but Toronto was hurting and needed a savior. They wanted Mahovlich to fill the bill, yet the kid just wouldn't seem to cooperate, the ingrate!

"When I came to Toronto," reminisced Frank recently, "they expected me to be Moses. They had no one else to look to and no one else to put the pressure on. I got it all."

As Mahovlich began his fourth NHL season, 1960-61, he had acquired a bad press reputation—he was moody and withdrawn, according to his clippings. Furthermore, The Big M was said to have no defensive abilities to speak of.

"There was a rumor that I couldn't play defense," snorted Frank over coffee one winter day. "How the hell could they say that when I was never given the chance?"

Despite growing rumbles against the young star, Frank had a brilliant season—his second "comeback" at the tender age of 23—, scoring 48 goals and 36 assists for 84 points. The fickle fans and press began to think that The Big M really was Moses, after all. And Chicago was reported to have offered $1 million for the services of Mahovlich.

"Toronto always expected too much of him," said Ranger general manager-coach Emile Francis. "The worst thing that happened to him was scoring 48 goals in a season so early in his career. The pressure was on him after that to do the same."

From 1962 through 1964 Frank helped spark the Leafs to three consecutive Stanley Cups, under turbulent and controversial coach "Punch" Imlach. But Frank's personal black cloud continued to dog him through the newsprint.

When Frank had a four-goal game one night, the press reminded their readers the next day that The Big M was really a "homer." Then, after scoring four goals in two games *away* at Boston Garden, Frank was accused of scoring all the time against "soft goaltending." And despite continued goal-scoring, Frank's relationship with the touchy Imlach seemed to grow cooler each season.

During 1964-65 Frank's scoring slipped and he was continuously booed on home ice. Finally, he suffered the first of what were later revealed to be nervous breakdowns, described as "deep depression and tension."

"If Toronto fans would appreciate his great talent and give him the cheers he deserves, instead of booing him, maybe the pressure wouldn't cook the guy," said Red Wing great Gordie Howe at the time.

But by then everyone knew that Frank Mahovlich was peculiar, different from the average hockey player—even his teammates couldn't understand the woeful-eyed winger.

"I played with Frank for eleven years," teammate Bob Baun said, "and I probably never said 22 words to the guy."

Pete Stemkowski, a former Toronto teammate, echoed Baun's sentiment:

"When we were in Toronto, you were lucky to get a hello from Frank."

Eventually Mahovlich returned to the lineup and to relative obscurity. That was another curious facet of The Big M's life—when he wasn't the best or the most disappointing or the sickest, he was virtually ignored by the press.

But the misunderstanding was to crop up again, ultimately leading to Frank's third "comeback."

In the middle of the 1967-68 season Mahovlich played an "outstanding" game, according to his supreme judge and arch critic, Imlach. The Leafs beat the Canadiens, 5-0, at Maple Leaf Gardens, and Frank's goal and two assists earned him "second star" category by broadcaster Foster Hewitt after the game.

Frank skated out on the ice when his name was called, no doubt expecting the normal round of applause. But there was scant applause. Instead, he was greeted with a vocal round of jeering and hooting from season ticket holders who had long ago decided that no matter what Big M did, it wasn't good enough.

Frank left the ice, his perpetually sad face set and motionless. After changing in silence, he went to the sleeping car that would carry the team to Detroit, and sat brooding. At 4 o'clock in the morning he arose, found the team physician, and was escorted to a hospital. Frank once more was reported to be suffering from "deep depression and tension," and was in the care of a psychiatrist, Dr. Allan Walters.

It was obvious by this time that Toronto bigwigs, primarily Imlach, would love to unload the problematic Mahovlich, but he had to play again and prove he was worth a trade. Frank did return, with improvement.

Early in March of 1968 Imlach found his buyer, and manipulated one of hockey's most spectacular trades. Mahovlich, Stemkowski, and rookie Garry Unger—plus the rights to then-retired defenseman Carl Brewer—would go to Detroit for high-scoring Norm Ullman, Floyd Smith, and talented young Paul Henderson. There were heated debates as to which team had gotten the better of the trade.

Red Fisher, sports editor of the Montreal *Star*, believed that Detroit had the edge, but naturally not because of Mahovlich: "This is a man of superior talent," said Fisher of The Big M, "but he is a disturbed and fretful character. The most valuable acquisition in the trade is Brewer."

And Punch made it painfully clear he was delighted to be rid of his troublesome left wing. "Hockey is mostly a streetcar named Desire. Sometimes Frank doesn't catch it."

Frank appeared at first to be a rusty streetcar in Detroit, but it was near the end of the season and he merely needed time to make his third NHL "comeback."

"It took about six months for me to get adjusted," he said. "You know, they'd heard all the Frank Mahovlich stories and they were wondering if they were true. And I was never the kind of guy who tried to sell myself."

Bill Gadsby, a former NHL defenseman who had played against Mahovlich, was named Detroit coach in 1968-69, and in a wise move, placed Frank at left wing on the great Howe-Delvecchio line.

Right away the line hit it off spectacularly. By March of 1969 the line was tops in league scoring, and Frank finished among the top 10 with 49 goals and 29 assists for 78 points. His performance was almost as good the next year, with 70 points. Frank was loose and happy, trading jokes and banter with his teammates. And Detroit loved him. It looked as though the bad days were all over.

But 1970-71 was bad, very bad for Detroit. The club

was riddled with dissension. Gadsby had long disappeared, replaced by Ned Harkness, former Cornell University coach with no NHL experience. Then, longtime Detroit general manager Sid Abel was fired, and Harkness was moved upstairs, replaced by coaching beginner and ex-defenseman Doug Barkley. The team worsened rapidly and steadily.

"I've never seen a situation crumble so quickly," said Frank. "It was no fun playing for a team and an organization that was that mixed up.

"Usually when a team fails, it happens gradually, but this collapse happened so fast. Everybody was unhappy there, even Gordie. There was a power struggle going on with management and we knew it had to affect us."

It affected Frank, all right. On January 13, 1971—just three days after his 33rd birthday—Mahovlich was traded to the Montreal Canadiens for Mickey Redmond, Guy Charron, and Bill Collins.

Everyone knew Frank had been happy for the first time in his life in Detroit, after the sorrowful years in Toronto. The big question was, would he revert to being moody and withdrawn in the "other" fickle Canadian NHL city, Montreal? His critics in Montreal would be almost as tough, if not more so, than his former Toronto hounds had been for 11 long years.

"Considering the situation in Detroit," Mahovlich said, "I guess I'm glad.

"Leaving Detroit was tough. I had two real good years there and enjoyed playing with the Wings, but I always wondered about Montreal . . . and I'm with Pete now."

Pete, of course, is Frank's light-hearted younger brother. The Mahovlich boys had been together a short while in Detroit, but Pete was traded in 1969 to the Canadiens. The fact that Pete was already at home in Montreal, and that the Canadiens team—like Detroit—had such great veterans as Jean Beliveau and Henri Richard to deflect curiosity from the reticent Frank were important pluses.

"When I came here," remembers Frank, "I saw that Pete wasn't just another player—he was a leader here and it made it easier for me to blend in."

Another big difference for the shy Mahovlich was the fact that he was immediately informed of the trade by Montreal general manager Sam Pollock, instead of finding out accidentally from a prying newsman, as he had when traded to Detroit by Toronto. Pollock even had an apartment ready for Frank and his wife when they arrived.

"It's just different here," explained Frank. "People still come up to me and I'm in the papers a lot, but they seem to be friendlier. If I have a bad game, no one gets down on me."

So big, misunderstood Frank Mahovlich entered his fourth, and maybe final, comeback. Although he scored a respectable 17 goals and 24 assists for 41 points in his short tenure with Montreal during the 1970-71 season, it was in the Stanley Cup playoffs that he really proved that he belonged in Montreal.

The Canadiens first upset the hockey world by beating the No. 1 rated Boston Bruins in the initial round of the playoffs, and Frank's seven goals were a big help. The Habs next galloped through the second round against Minnesota four games to two, to finally face the tough, much-improved Chicago Black Hawks.

It was a hard and grueling series. Montreal lost the first two games and then came from behind to win the next two. Chicago took game No. 5, but Montreal once again tied the series in the sixth game, coming from behind to win, 4-3.

In that sixth game Frank got a once-in-a-lifetime opportunity: the first penalty shot awarded in the history of the Stanley Cup, on Chicago's ace goalie Tony Esposito. Frank blew it!

"When he (Esposito) retreated, I tried to blow the puck past him. It was a good shot, but I didn't get it high enough. Perhaps I reacted too quickly, should have let him get deeper into his net."

That mistake may have been the only one Frank made during the whole series; he certainly didn't let his former depression get the best of him. The Habs won it all and Frank broke the Stanley Cup goal record with 14, and tied Phil Esposito's playoff point total with 27.

And as always, when the victorious Canadiens were feted in Montreal after the win, it was rookie Canadiens goaltender Ken Dryden and impish, exhibitionist brother Pete who got all the ink. But Frank no longer cared; he was happy.

Frank was chosen alternate captain of the Canadiens

and to him it was a sign that he is really accepted by his teammates.

"It's the first time I've ever been chosen for anything," he said proudly. "They showed that they respected me. It's a nice feeling to have."

The media began to criticize again when Frank's scoring slipped after a hot start last year but after almost 15 years in the NHL Frank seems unmoved by the fickle printed word. He calmly scored his 20th against his former team, the Leafs, on January 1, and quieted the wagging tongues.

By the end of last season Frank had collected 43 goals and 53 assists for 96 points to lead Montreal in scoring. The total was good enough to place The Big M sixth in the NHL race and leave Frank with a minimum of bitterness about the past, unless, perhaps, Imlach is mentioned.

"What's the point in crying over spilt milk?" philosophized the now composed and nonchalant Mahovlich. "Sure I could say some ifs and buts, but it wouldn't do me any good. What happened then, happened then, and there is no point in rehashing."

Frank now has a prospering travel agency in Toronto and last Christmas he sent a card to a Toronto neighbor, noted Canadian artist A. J. Casson, mentioning that he would be happy to trade hockey lessons for painting lessons!

From a young man who was obviously deeply hurt by each barb and boo ever thrown his way, Frank has become a self-confident and assured veteran who knows what he wants and is unconcerned with public approval or approbation.

Frank once expressed the intense desire to be a 20-year man; but recently when asked that question, he responded, again with all the unconcern of one never troubled by doubt:

"Oh, I guess I'll play as long as I want to. . . ."

The Big M of today reminds one of a Matthew Arnold poem aptly entitled, "Self-Dependence":

"Resolve to be thyself; and know that he
Who finds himself, loses his misery."

PETER MAHOVLICH At the height of the Montreal
Canadiens' Stanley Cup victory celebration at City Hall
on May 19, 1971, a glint-eyed young man built along the
generous dimensions of a Clydesdale stallion walked
over to the tiny Mayor Jean Drapeau of Montreal.

The 6-4, 210-pound behemoth, who happened to be
walking around in bare feet, then delivered a hearty
thwack against the mayor's back. "I heard," Peter Mahovlich said to the startled mayor, "that you sleep in your
shoes."

Few people in the world are capable of taking the
liberties that Peter Mahovlich enjoyed that afternoon. He
kissed the hands of a dozen women on City Hall steps, he
drank wine while crossing his legs barefoot in the recep-
tion room and he insisted that Mayor Drapeau inspect
teammate Henri Richard's sparkling white shoes.

Perhaps more startling was the fact that only three
years ago Peter might have been tossed out of Montreal's
City Hall as an impostor as he was cast out of Detroit as
an impostor hockey player with the Red Wings. Yet now
he still was being hailed as the genuine—with all deference
to goalie Ken Dryden—hero of the Canadiens' arresting
Stanley Cup triumph and the man who experienced a Mr.
Hyde to Dr. Jekyll transformation that converted him
from a hockey flop to a star.

Peter's 61 point total of 1970-71 was bettered last
season when he scored 35 goals and 32 assists for 67
points. Once again he proved he was far from the flop of
yesteryear.

As flops go, Mahovlich once was among the biggest—
both physically and spiritually. The 26-year-old kid brother of Frank "Big M" Mahovlich, Peter moved through the
Detroit Red Wing chain until he reached the NHL in
1965-66. In 37 games over a two-season span he scored a
grand total of one goal. After 82 games he had nine goals,

and in May 1969 the Red Wings management fingered Peter as a fraud.

"Pete Mahovlich is a con artist," said Jimmy Skinner, the Wings' chief scout who was appearing on Dave Diles WXYZ Detroit radio show. "He won't work. He's riding on his brother's reputation. I drafted him for the organization but I hope he's traded."

Others close to the Wings pointed out that Peter was more interested in laughs than goals, so it was with a considerable sigh of relief that Detroit traded Mahovlich to Montreal with Bart Crashley for Garry Monahan and Doug Piper.

"Obviously," says Peter, "I didn't get a fair shake in Detroit. I went to training camp that first year and worked as hard as I could. I had the highest point production in the exhibition games, made the club, and then the season opened and I never saw the ice."

With that in mind it's hard to imagine that Peter scored 35 goals for the Canadiens in 1970-71 and five vital goals during the 1971 Stanley Cup finals against Chicago. But the fact remains that the big broth of a boy from Timmins, Ontario, was consummately unspectacular in 1969-70, his first season in Montreal. He yo-yoed back and forth between Les Canadiens and Les Voyageurs of the American League.

"He had bad knees," says John Ferguson, the ex-Canadiens left wing who was to play a decisive role in the making of Mahovlich. "He never really got started and he never got mad."

It was the total lack of belligerency on Peter's part that mystified Ferguson. According to Fergie, everyone on the opposition should be hated and hated hard. What's more, a mammoth like Mahovlich should be bulldozing everyone in sight instead of acting like Florence Nightingale, which is the way Ferguson interpreted Peter's style. Finally Ferguson decided he could contain himself no more.

"I met Fergie one day," says Mahovlich, "and he said 'Come with me, kid. I want to talk to you.' And I went. We sat down and he said he couldn't understand why, when I was the biggest man in the National Hockey League, I was playing the way I was. He told me I should be skating right over the top of people, instead of skirting around them. He said I had nothing to fear from anybody

in the league so I should be playing that way—
aggressively, going after people."

Peter scored nine goals and eight assists for 17 points in
36 NHL games during the 1969-70 season with Montreal.
Ferguson, the tutor, watched and wasn't satisfied. Mahovlich, he believed, would have to be even meaner.
Another lecture was in order.

"I spent a week with Peter at a summer hockey school
in 1970," Ferguson recalls. "I kept telling him he should
be still more aggressive."

Mahovlich listened as Ferguson's eyes burned fiercely.
"You've got the size and ability. Get mad and start leaning on people. You gotta hate those other guys."

When Peter showed up at the Canadiens training camp
in September 1970 his teammates noticed a boisterousness
about him that bothers people the way a runaway car
disturbs the cop in the street. Ferguson, however, was all
smiles.

"Peter got the message," said Fergie.

From the start of the season Mahovlich's penalty minutes climbed like the temperature gauge in an overheated
car. During a game at the Vancouver Coliseum he traded
punches with Canucks goalie Dunc Wilson and so angered
a fan that the spectator leaped out of his seat, ran to the
penalty box, and berated Mahovlich. Fortunately Peter
does have his fans and one of them happened to be a
female who promptly chased after the irate male and
punched him directly in the chops.

Peter managed to distill a combination of both anger
and humor as the 1970-71 season neared its end and he
piled up a total of 181 penalty minutes. During a game
against St. Louis at the Montreal Forum Peter attacked
former Blues defenseman Jim Roberts, who later became
Peter's teammate, and then clashed with center Garry
Unger.

The St. Louis bench needled Peter for his manhandling
of Roberts but Mahovlich later explained, "I'm not the
best fighter in the world but that guy is handy with his
stick and you can't let him get away with it."

Seconds after the Mahovlich-Roberts bout had been
stopped, Unger charged at Peter but Mahovlich never
forgot that Unger was his buddy once in Detroit. The
Gulliverian left wing merely put his massive right hand

over Unger's blond mane and held the St. Louis forward by the hair until Unger said uncle.

"That's the second time Peter had a great chance to hit me and didn't," Unger laughed. "We were good friends at Detroit."

But Peter had no friends on the Boston Bruins and proved it by the manner in which he manhandled them in the opening round of the 1971 Stanley Cup playoffs.

With Boston leading the best-of-seven series, three games to two, it was Mahovlich who led the Canadiens to a mighty 8-3 victory over the Bruins in the sixth game of the series with a splendid job of penalty-killing, two key goals, and a fight with superstar Bobby Orr that removed both players from the game. Mahovlich was cuffing Orr to and fro until Boston forward Johnny McKenzie rushed in and belted Peter from behind.

"I really didn't welcome McKenzie's involvement," said Peter. "I was doing okay against Orr, who doesn't need help in fighting."

When Mahovlich and Orr sat themselves down in the penalty box Peter cooled his fury long enough to throw a few ice cubes to Orr so that the Bruin could refresh himself.

"Fights flare up quickly," Peter explained later, "but we cool off just as fast. Besides, Orr was probably as thirsty as I was."

Peter rekindled his hatred of the Bruins in the seventh and final game of the series at Boston Garden. He was the architect of a first-period goal that put Montreal ahead to stay in the first period and was ubiquitous throughout the game in which Montreal won, 4-2, scoring one of sports' most astonishing upsets. In the gloom-enshrouded Boston dressing room, Orr singled out Peter as the key Canadien.

"He was a great player for them all the way," said Orr. "He was doing something for them all the time on his line, killing penalties, yelling from the bench—everything."

Trailing Chicago, two games to none, the Canadiens appeared on the ropes in the third game of the finals until Peter scored the first goal and Frank scored the tying and clinching goals in a 4-2 Canadiens win. One of the spectators in the audience was Peter, Sr., Mahovlich, who was visiting Montreal for the first time since he had arrived in Canada in 1929 as an immigrant from Croatia, Yugoslavia. The elder Mahovlich entered the Canadiens dressing room after the game and headed straight for Peter, Jr., and shook his hand. "Now," said Junior to his dad, "go over there and congratulate the little guy." He was pointing at Frank who stands four inches shorter than Pete at 6-0.

Chicago appeared quite capable of winning the Stanley Cup in the sixth match after taking a three-two lead in games. The Black Hawks led 3-2 as late as the five-minute mark of the third period when Frank Mahovlich tied the score. With almost nine minutes gone in the period Peter was on the ice killing a Canadiens penalty when Bobby Hull of Chicago attempted to bounce the puck off the boards.

Frank Mahovlich intercepted the puck and sighted Peter who was uncovered. "The pass was right on the money," said Peter. "I walked in, faked Tony Esposito away from the post and lifted the shot high on the short side." The goal enabled Montreal to emerge with a 4-3 victory and a three-three tie in the series.

And while all this was going on Peter marauded up and down the ice flattening Black Hawks like tenpins. To the distant observer it appeared that Mahovlich's terrorizing tactics were delivered without harm to his massive superstructure but Peter confessed that ever since he had adapted the Ferguson meanness policy he, himself, had suffered, particularly in his elbows.

"The fact is," Mahovlich explained, "a guy like me can't go around banging his elbow and not feel it. My problem is that my elbows are slightly smaller than a bread box, but they're not knobby little things like Fergie's elbows. I thought I solved the problem by having a manufacturer make some oversized pads that are so big I figure Yvan Cournoyer can use 'em for shin guards. But even they started to crack."

Fortunately for Montreal, Peter did not crack in the 1971 Cup final game against Chicago. He remained superhot against the Black Hawks and cool with his teammates, reassuring them even when they trailed 2-0 in the game.

At one point in the second period Mahovlich and Eric Nesterenko of Chicago needled each other into roughing penalties. As Peter skated to the penalty box he turned to teammate Jacques Lemaire. "Don't worry," he said, "I need a rest. We'll be all right."

At 11:18 of the period and Chicago ahead, 2-0, Lemaire bombed a long shot past goalie Esposito. Then Henri Richard tied the score for Montreal and Richard scored again in the third period to put the Canadiens ahead, 3-2, which is precisely how the score ended, and Montreal won the Stanley Cup.

Sipping champagne in the dressing room Peter bubbled over the comeback. "You know," he said, "at no time did we ever feel down in the game, even when we were behind by two. We just made up our minds to hit them and that's what we did. And then Lemaire got us started."

A day later Mahovlich was at the head of the Canadiens victory parade before the biggest crowd in Montreal history. Significantly, the man riding alongside Peter was John Ferguson, who later was to announce his retirement.

"That guy," said Peter, "has been the biggest help. Not only in my attitude, but he went into the corners and set me up time after time."

With Ferguson gone, Peter has had some trouble retaining his white heat attitude. But when he does, he need only remember Fergie's words in the Vancouver dressing room three seasons ago as Mahovlich bounced his shin pads off the wall.

"STAY MAD, PETER! STAY MAD!"

JOHNNY McKENZIE There are many who believe that 35-year-old Johnny "Pie" McKenzie, more than any other player, epitomized the heart and style of the Boston Bruins.

Tough.

There are others who insist that the impish looking right wing from High River, Alberta now will assure Philadelphia's success in the WHA.

Take your pick. Whatever it is there is no doubting the impact that McKenzie has made on the new league, as player-coach of the Blazers, McKenzie will be as popular as he was in Beantown.

In 1970 McKenzie was voted the Most Popular Player on the Bruins. Look around Boston and you'll see little kids wearing Johnny Pie sweatshirts. He's come a long way from those doldrum days in Buffalo (American League) in 1963. "That's where I got the 'Pie' nickname," says McKenzie. "A guy named Gerry Melnyk gave it to me. He was on Buffalo, too, and I guess he figured my round face looked like a pie so I've been Pie ever since."

He's also been murder to opposition goalies—22 goals and 47 assists for 69 points in 77 games last season—as well as enemy skaters.

In the 1969 Stanley Cup playoff between Boston and Montreal the then Canadiens' coach Claude Ruel grated over McKenzie's roughhouse style and denounced him to the press as "yellow." That was neither the first nor last blast leveled at the Bruin. Brad Park, the Rangers' gifted young defenseman, verbally tarred and feathered McKenzie in Park's book "Play the Man."

Said Brad of Pie: "McKenzie's bag is running at people *from behind*. No player really objects to getting hit straight on, but when a guy rams you from behind that's bad news."

Like him or not, McKenzie comes by his toughness naturally. For years he spent the off-season as a rodeo rider in his native Alberta. "The most I ever won," says Pie, "was $150 in a wild-cow milking contest. I never did make $500 in a season which would have qualified me for the Cowboys' Protective Association. But I did get to believe that rodeo cowboys are the best-conditioned athletes in all sports."

Curiously, McKenzie was not a particularly high-scorer during his earlier NHL days with Chicago, Detroit, and New York. It was the trade to Boston that brought on the Pie metamorphosis. "In New York, the Rangers stressed a more finesse type of game. I didn't have that kind of finesse. When I got to the Bruins I knew I could skate as well as any of them and my confidence developed."

So did his pugnaciousness. "The reason I fight on the ice," said McKenzie, "is the will to win. Our game is a bodily game. Brothers play against each other and fight.

It's part of the game. To win in hockey you have to be physical." And we'll win in Philly."

Just how long McKenzie can retain his effectiveness— as a player-coach will depend in large part on how long McKenzie can continue his effervescent sprinting and "disturbing" tactics with the opposition.

During a game against Toronto in January 1971 Pie suffered an unusually painful shoulder separation. At his age, and with his style, injuries like that set a man thinking.

"No doubt," he admits, "I'm more conscious of injuries but not when I'm on the ice. The minute you start getting shy you're going to get hurt. I still think I hit as hard as I always did."

WHA opponents will be inclined to agree.

RICHARD MARTIN At first it seemed hard to believe; comparing a raw rookie with such arresting goal-scorers as Maurice "Rocket" Richard, Gordie Howe, Phil Esposito, and Bobby Hull. Yet there was Richard "Rick" Martin of the Buffalo Sabres, blazing his way through the 1971-72 NHL season, scoring goals as fast as the best of them.

Surely, it was thought, Martin would burn himself out by mid-season. Never, the experts insisted, would he equal the rookie record set only a year earlier by his teammate, Gil Perreault. But Martin not only erased Perreault's record by February 1972, he went on to score an astonishing 44 goals and 30 assists for 74 points, leading the Sabres in scoring.

How, then, could this be possible for a 21-year-old left wing who was virtually as unknown as the other side of Venus just a year and a half ago?

The answer is that Martin, whether it was realized then or not, owns the best armament for breaking goal-scoring records since the invention of Bobby Hull. "He has the best shot in the NHL," says Bernie Geoffrion, who once had the best shot in the NHL when he played for the Montreal Canadiens. "Maybe he has the best shot I've ever seen."

Geoffrion is not alone in his appraisal. George "Punch" Imlach, the man who drafted Martin, shares the sentiments. "Martin is the best goal-scorer I've ever coached," said Imlach. "And I've had Jean Beliveau and Frank Mahovlich on my teams. This kid is one of those players who has special gifts, little skills for producing goals that only a very few players ever have. He doesn't have the stamina of a Mahovlich or Beliveau, but he can score more ways. He can overpower goalies with his slapshot, hit with his wrist shot or his backhand, which is a dandy, and in close, in the traffic, he's got just the right touch for doing the right thing. You never know what he's going to do and I don't think he does, which makes him tough to stop."

Perhaps most typical of Martin's goals was the 39th red light he illuminated last season to break Perreault's record. It was in a Saturday night game against the Toronto Maple Leafs. Martin was camped about 15 in front of Leafs goalie Jacques Plante, a bit closer to Plante's right side. Sabres defenseman Al Hamilton had the puck near the blue line and spotted Martin. He skimmed a quick pass and what followed was best described by Southam News Service columnist Jim Coleman of Toronto.

"The puck," wrote Coleman, "simply didn't have the opportunity to enjoy the pause that refreshes. As soon as the puck touched the blade of his stick Martin propelled it into the lower corner of the net, to Plante's right.

"Some observers might describe the scoring drive as a golf shot. It would be more accurate to describe it as a cricket stroke. Martin caught the puck on the half-volley and drove it out of sight. As a matter of fact, the puck travelled to swiftly to be discerned clearly by the human eye."

So stirring was the goal that everyone in Buffalo Memorial Auditorium rose as one to give Martin a deafening ovation. He was patted, whacked, and otherwise congratulated by his teammates and even the supposedly reserved gentlemen of the press applauded.

Many in the audience actually believed that Martin would score 50 goals in a season to join such luminaries as Richard, Hull, Geoffrion, and Esposito. Martin, of course, didn't reach that glorious plateau, but then again, this is another year and it is something to think about—which he does.

"A lot of people talk about me scoring 50 goals some-time," said Martin. "If I make it, it will be super. But if I don't, it won't be any great letdown. Last season I set my sights on 39 goals but even that wasn't my dominant thought. All I wanted to do was play well in every game."

The son of a French-Canadian mother and a French-Swiss father, Martin was born in Montreal but learned to skate in Hull, Ontario, where his family moved when he was four. His father was coaching his first hockey team when Richard was eight and Martin responded with 38 goals *in his first three games*. His progress in the next few years betrayed the cloak of a someday superstar—top scorer in both bantam and midget leagues, and in one game he scored 12 goals.

"By the time I was 13 years old," he said, "I knew I could make it as a hockey pro."

The test would be an audition with the Montreal Junior Canadiens, one of Canada's most powerful Junior A amateur clubs from whom came such stars as Perreault, Jacques Laperriere, and Guy Lapointe, to name a few. His production was activated enough to inspire the NHL Canadiens to hope that other big-league clubs would by-pass Martin in the 1971 NHL draft but he was too desirable to be overlooked.

"All I wanted," said Martin, "was to be claimed by a team that would give me a chance to show what I could do and play in the NHL if I showed enough. As it turned out Buffalo was just right for me."

Martin's critics, and there have been a few, downgrade him for his lack of defensive vigilance and the fact that he has a playboy image, whether it's deserved or not. Most observers insist that the former is more accurate than the latter.

"I'm not a big liver," said Martin in defense of his life-style, "and I don't pass myself off as one. People always try to give you some image you're not. I've worked too hard to get here just to throw it all away on big living."

The Sabres management is not really all that concerned about *how* Richard Martin lives as long as the big number

While the Boston Bruins and New York Rangers were playing for the Stanley Cup, the Milton Massachusetts Warriors, representing Boston, were playing the Columbia Lions, representing New York, for the street hockey championship. Steve Anderson of Milton (far left) takes a shot at goalie Bob Murphy. Like the Stanley Cup, the street hockey championship landed in Massachusetts as Milton won the two-game series, 14–11 and 8–6.   *(Photo by RICK MEISNER)*

Detroit Red Wings' center Red Berenson lifts the puck over prone Pittsburgh Penguins' goaltender Jim Rutherford for a score.   *(UPI)*

Boston Bruins' all-star center Phil Esposito cleanly beats Montreal goalie Ken Dryden, as Bruins' right wing John McKenzie and Montreal's defenseman Jaques Laperriere look on.   (UPI)

Bobby Orr, Phil Esposito, and Don Awrey enjoy a frivolous moment in the Boston Bruins' dressing room.   (UPI)

Pittsburgh Penguins' center Syl Apps raises stick jubilantly after putting both puck and Los Angeles Kings' defenseman Harry Howell into the net. *(UPI)*

Pittsburgh Penguins' Eddie "The Entertainer" Shack is obviously shaken after being slammed into the boards by Montreal Canadiens' defenseman Guy Lapointe. *(UPI)*

New York Rangers' right wing Rod Gilbert looks for help as he is confronted at the blue line by Boston Bruins' ace Bobby Orr. *(UPI)*

Montreal Canadiens' forward Frank Mahovlich and Minnesota North Stars' defenseman Barry Gibbs seem to be about to clobber Minnesota Goalie Cesare Maniago. Actually Mahovlich is raising his stick in celebration after putting the puck past Maniago and the frustrated Gibbs. *(UPI)*

Boston Bruins' Golden Boy Bobby Orr isn't about to let anyone play with "his" puck. Here he avoids a poke-check from New York Rangers' left wing Vic Hadfield and stick-handles up ice. New York's Brad Park and Boston's Derek Sanderson watch in awe. *(UPI)*

Boston's small but tough forward John McKenzie leaves his feet to throw a crunching bodycheck at then Buffalo Sabres' center Phil Goyette. *(UPI)*

Chicago's Stan Mikita knocks the puck past Montreal goalie Ken Dryden, who later received the Calder Trophy for 1971–72 as NHL Rookie of the Year. *(UPI)*

A score by Toronto's crack shooter Paul Henderson is greeted by incredulous looks from beaten Ranger netminder Gilles Vellemure and defenseman Jim Neilson. *(UPI)*

A scoring bid by slick New York Rangers' center Jean Ratelle is foiled by Minnesota defenseman Doug Mohns. Goaltender Gump Worsley keeps a close eye on the action.
(UPI)

Montreal's big Peter Mahovlich fires wrist shot wide of cage manned by Chicago Black Hawks' all-star goalie Tony Esposito. *(UPI)*

Chicago stars Bobby Hull, Tony Esposito, and Stan Mikita relax in dressing room after a light workout prior to a Stanley Cup game in April, 1972. *(UPI)*

Minnesota North Stars' goalie Gump Worsley probably wishes he was wearing a mask, as shot by Buffalo's Larry Keenan appears to be headed for his mouth. But puck sailed wide of Gump and net. *(UPI)*

seven scores goals the way he did last year. If he does, Rocket Richard, Gordie Howe, and Bobby Hull had better create some more room in the Hockey Hall of Fame.

STAN MIKITA There was the net. Six feet wide, four feet high. Empty. Very empty.

There was the clock. Two-two. Rangers vs. Chicago. Sixth game, 1971 Stanley Cup semifinals. Second sudden-death overtime.

There was Stan Mikita with the puck on his stick. He was not far from the net. In fact, he was so close Mikita would put that shot in 100 out of 100 times during a practice.

Mikita, 32-year-old Black Hawks center, shot the puck and missed the part of the goal that counts. Later, during the third sudden-death overtime, Peter Stemkowski won the game for New York.

To those who have watched the Czech-born Mikita in his often-brilliant 13-year National Hockey League career the vignette betrayed a pathetic symbolism; for this was no longer the Stan Mikita of old. He had become in his hockey "middle-age" a different man. He no longer was the greatest.

At one point he had been atop the summit. He led the league in scoring four times but last season Mikita was 17th on the list. He won the Hart Trophy and Lady Byng Trophy simultaneously two years in succession but last year he couldn't even make the All-Star Team.

More than anything, Mikita seemed to have lost the killer instinct that would have enabled him to sink his stick into the Rangers' jugular with leonine ease last spring.

This phenomenon—the metamorphosis of athletes—is as old as the first ice skate but the reasons for such a change are infinite and often puzzling. In Mikita's case two vital developments appear to have transformed him from a terror to tranquil skater who may or may not be potent on any given night.

The most obvious is the indisputable fact that he suffered a back injury against Montreal on February 2, 1969, which has dramatically altered his cerebral let alone his center ice style.

The less obvious fact is that the man christened Stanislas Gvoth in his native Sokolce, Czechoslovakia, is a mature married man. Many mature fathers who play hockey for a living discover at a certain point in their careers that there is more than scoring goals to live for; there *is* more to life.

"Maybe," said a Chicago Black Hawks teammate, "Stan really doesn't give that much of a damn about hockey anymore. Maybe."

Supposing that *were* the case. Who could blame him after the agony that followed Mikita's fateful collision with the Canadiens more than three years ago? Certainly Stan himself has riveted the incident in his mind and nothing can dislodge it anymore.

"I was cross-checked twice from behind," said Mikita. "Suddenly, something snapped in my back. Just what it was I couldn't say. No vertebrae were broken or damaged. And when I try to find out precisely what it was no specific term can explain the injury. But, to me, it was just plain hell."

Significantly, in the season prior to his injury Mikita scored his second consecutive Triple Crown (Art Ross, Lady Byng, and Hart Trophies). Subsequently, he continued playing after hospitalization although close friends such as teammate Lou Angotti couldn't imagine how he did it.

Once Angotti visited Mikita in the hospital and found his buddy virtually immobile. Stan was fearful of swerving an inch to either side of the bed. But in time he was released and appeared to have made the adjustment. Last season Mikita managed to score 26 goals and 39 assists for 65 points, fourth best on Chicago.

"I like to think I learned to live with my bad back," he said. "There actually isn't much difference. I skate just as fast as I ever did. Maybe I'm not quite as durable. When we run into a stretch when we have four games in five nights I just can't spend as much time on the ice during a shift."

The perplexing aspect of Mikita's troublesome back is

that its agony-production is as changeable as the weather. There are nights when Stan might just as well have remained in bed and then there are other nights when he's the holy terror of old.

Still, others wonder about Stan's attitude. There is a suspicion that, more than ever, he is playing for the paycheck. Less gentle types insist he has shot his load as a star and now is coasting. At one point in his career it would have been unthinkable for the Black Hawks to trade Mikita. Now, who knows.

Stan realizes that manager Tommy Ivan would not be ultra-sensitive about trading Mikita even though Stan was developed in the Black Hawks' farm system and never played for another NHL club.

Still, it's hard to believe that Stan Mikita would wear anything but a Black Hawks jersey. This is the man who went from puck's bad boy to the double-Byng-winner, who perfected the curved stick to such a degree that the banana-blade became a vogue, and who helped make Chicago a respectable hockey team.

Whether Mikita now can lead the Bobby Hull-less Hawks is a question that can be answered best by an X-ray machine and those privy to Stan's innermost thoughts.

There are those who will never forget that spring night in Manhattan when he missed the open net and the Black Hawks blew a hockey game.

"I was never expecting the puck," Stan explained. "When I found it on my stick, I just sent it in the general direction of the net. I fired much too fast."

That happens.

But, then, a reporter recalled the abject look of despair on Mikita's face moments later during a lull in the play. He asked whether this was one of the most discouraging moments in his life.

"Guys are dying in Vietnam," said Mikita. "How can I be disappointed?"

It was a mature answer from a mature man who knows what pain is all about. One can only hope this pain does not remove his artistry from the NHL scene it has enriched so many years.

BOBBY ORR In the past it was Eddie Shore, Maurice "The Rocket" Richard, Gordie Howe, and Bobby Hull. In the seventies, the dominant hockey player is Bobby Orr of the Boston Bruins, a defenseman who is so good at scoring he finished right behind teammate Phil Esposito in the 1971-72 point race.

Nothing says it better about the 24-year-old native of Parry Sound, Ontario, than the trophies he has collected. In 1972, for example, he won the Hart Trophy as the National Hockey League's most valuable player for the third straight season—the first time this ever has been accomplished. He also won the Norris Trophy as the NHL's best defenseman and thus was the first ever to win the Norris five consecutive years.

In addition he was voted to the First All-Star Team and now has won at least one trophy in each of his six professional seasons. But perhaps most important, Orr is the sole reason why the Bruins have dominated the NHL in the past year, and defeated the Rangers in the 1972 Stanley Cup finals.

"The difference between New York and Boston," said Gus Kyle who played defense for both clubs, "is Orr. If you take him away from the Bruins the Rangers would win the Cup."

For a while the Rangers thought they'd be able to face an Orr-less Bruins last May. Bobby had injured his left knee late in the season and faced the prospect of surgery when the playoffs were over. There was a possibility that the knee would be too painful for him to play against New York.

Yet when the puck was dropped for the opening face-off Orr took his position on defense and went on to play his usual spectactular game despite the pain. "I'd like to be hurt as bad as he was," said Rangers defenseman Brad Park, "and play that well."

Orr's brilliance reached new heights in candlepower during the fourth game of the Stanley Cup finals at Madison Square Garden. With Boston leading the series, 2-1, it appeared that the Rangers would make a comeback on their home ice and tie the round. But Orr scored two goals and assisted on the third as the Bruins captured the game, 3-2.

"Bobby is something," said goalie Ed Johnston, "isn't he?"

He is all things to all people, and not all that complimentary either. But as a hockey player, Orr is all star. Bobby himself may not admit that he commands the Bruins ship and that when he decides to take charge the game tilts in Boston's favor, but others know this to be true.

"Orr is so great," said teammate Derek Sanderson, "because he doesn't consciously try to take charge; he just does it, automatically."

"Even when he's not moving well," said Rangers captain Vic Hadfield, "Orr still controls the play."

During the regular 1971-72 season he scored 37 goals and 80 assists for 117 points, second only to Phil Esposito. But respected critics don't consider the two in the same class; Orr is alone, well ahead of Esposito. He is the only Boston athlete who can be compared with Ted Williams.

"If a hockey player could bat .400," wrote columnist Harold Kaese of the Boston *Globe*, "Bobby Orr would be the man. He is a master of his craft, a virtuoso. Ted Williams, the brash one, was a more exciting sports personality than Bobby Orr, the shy one, but in their professions they are comparable performers."

"In my 36 years in the NHL," said Bruins manager Milt Schmidt, "Bobby is the greatest player I have ever seen in the past, the greatest player at present, and if anyone greater should show up, I just hope the Good Lord has me around here to see him and let him be a Bruin."

Orr not only has taken on Messianic qualities for the Bruins, but for the NHL as well. In an era when big-league hockey is spreading its wings to new areas of North America, Orr remains the most saleable commodity the shinny moguls have to offer. And nobody knows it better than Orr's attorney Al Eagleson of Toronto.

"Bobby is the only player who can help out the low-drawing teams in the NHL," said Eagleson. "For example, in Oakland, Orr played there on a Sunday night and drew 10,500. St. Louis came there on a Wednesday and drew 3,000. In Los Angeles, Orr drew 12,700, the next night against St. Louis the crowd was only 7,200. Vancouver's manager says he could sell an extra 30,000-40,000 tickets when Orr is in town."

This continental adulation of Orr does not stop at the end of the hockey season. Two years ago Bobby visited Vancouver and, within ten hours, conducted several interviews, appeared on a talk show, spoke at a luncheon, and then conducted a three-hour autograph session with kids. When asked about his position in the prime center of the NHL limelight, Orr replied:

"I never think of myself as an idol. I'm a hockey player. I enjoy the hockey. The money? I never think about becoming a millionaire, or anything. When I quit, it will be because I don't enjoy it anymore. Of course, sometimes it's a little bit tough. You sign your name and you're polite, when all you want to do is get away by yourself. But they won't let you go. I sign autographs until I go batty."

Orr receives an average of 5,000 letters each week during the hockey season. They've come in such droves that a Boston newspaper once devoted two full pages to nothing but letters to Bobby Orr for most of the hockey season.

Despite his impact on the hockey world, Orr the person has often appeared aloof and occasionally surly. The fuss and fanfare have affected him a lot more than his friends and agents care to admit.

"Throughout it all," observed author Tom Dowling, "Orr remains remote and circumspect, a little abashed at all the furor unloosed in his name, like some medieval monk whose pious lifework has inadvertently overturned the status quo of which he is a contented member."

The Orr paradox was never better exemplified than in the 1970-71 season when *Sports Illustrated* selected him as its "Sportsman of the Year." Yet in the article, author Jack Olsen depicts episodes which question the true nature of sportsmanship. At one point Olsen reports that Orr cut off another motorist while driving. Then Bobby gunned his car the wrong way on a one-way street and later berated a *maitre d'hotel* at a restaurant.

Whatever his off-ice behavior, Orr's deportment on the ice cannot be questioned in terms of his abilities. When he entered the NHL at age 18 he displayed the strong skating, mighty shot, unwavering courage, and keen instincts that comprise the superstar. What's more, he played a vital role in changing hockey from a bush-league low-paying sport into one of the higher-salaried team games.

Until Bobby Orr came along, nobody but nobody in professional hockey—and that includes the super-dupers like Gordie Howe and Bobby Hull—earned more than $40,000.

Orr, with the help from his attorney-advisor R. Alan Eagleson, changed that. Bobby now is collecting $1,000,-000 spread over five years and has helped lift the salaries of his colleagues in the process. Friends and foes alike toast Orr like no other athlete in their profession.

"He is," said Bobby Hull, "the greatest young hockey player that's come along since I've been here and that's 16 years. He controls the puck. If he doesn't have the room to skate with it he'll give it to a teammate and then bust to get it back. Most guys, after they've given it up, will just watch it go. Bobby takes off and when he hits your blue line he's streaking."

Dave Keon of Toronto added: "Orr's success comes down to his mastery of the basics. He's so quick. He anticipates extremely well. He wants to be good and he has great natural ability. The combination is hard to beat."

The anti-Orr school of thinking has it that he really is overrated on the grounds that the Bruins make Orr rather than the vice being versa. One such relevant opinion was submitted by right wing Ron Ellis, a cerebral member of the Toronto Maple Leafs.

"Orr," said Ellis, "no doubt is in his own league. But the players he's with are a powerhouse, and they make him look good. He makes a beautiful pass, but he has guys with him who know what to do with it."

Another dissenting vote was submitted by forward Rosaire Paiement who twice clouted Orr in fights in the same game. "The first time," Paiement recalled, "I tried to check him and I knocked him down with my elbow. He came right after me. . . . I didn't expect anything to happen but then he tried to sucker me; he threw the first punch, which is normally the big one, but he missed me completely. I didn't miss him. I got him with a right under the left eye and he was cut pretty good. In the third period he jumped me in the corner. He's proud; he wanted to fight again. Especially in Boston, he's got to come back again. This time I cut him good on the same eye."

Opponents see all things in Orr but the best of them all, Gordie Howe, believes the essence of Bobby's superiority is his leg strength.

"He's got the legs," Howe explained. "He's also got a good attitude, plenty of desire and he always hustles. He's also an awfully nice kid. In the summer of 1968 I had my two boys with me on a promotional trip to Bobby's hometown, Parry Sound, Ontario, and Bobby was dressed in a white shirt and tie. As soon as the festivities were over we went to his house and he changed into a sweatshirt.

"It was the one which had a Gordie Howe crest on the front. My boys like that."

Unconsciously Bobby's favorite word is "super." This is perfectly natural in view of his hockey-playing efforts. "Orr," says New York *Post* columnist Larry Merchant, "is at least hockey's sixth dimension. He is one of those rare athletes who revolutionizes his game as Babe Ruth did, as Bill Russell did. Bobby Jones once said of Jack Nicklaus, 'He plays a game with which I am not familiar.' Orr plays hockey in a way that makes old-timers feel like dinosaurs, too."

Orr's closest competitor for sheer all-round superiority is Brad Park, but Park readily concedes the edge. "There's a standing joke on the Rangers," said Park. "The guys tell me I better hurry up if I'm going to catch up with Bobby Orr; but they all know that I'll never catch up."

And if Park won't, nobody will.

BRAD PARK Few professional athletes ever have exposed themselves to more anger from the enemy than New York Rangers defenseman Brad Park, and all because he decided to become an author as well as the second-best backliner in the world.

Park, a pleasant, 24-year-old Toronto native who resembles Huckleberry Finn in style and temperament, wrote a book called "Play the Man" in which he devotes an entire chapter to analyzing the Boston Bruins as a team and individually. Many of his observations were uncomplimentary.

He likens the Bruins to a schoolyard bully who will push the smaller types around until someone stands up to him. He indicts players such as Phil Esposito ("He likes to run at people from behind") and, as a result, has been the target of Boston players off and on the ice. Even some of the Rangers have quietly resented the book on the grounds that it inspired the Bruins to attack the Rangers with even greater venom.

But Park never backed away. He stood up to the Bruins and stood by his book. "It was honest," said Brad, "and I said what I had to say. I knew the Bruins would be unhappy but I didn't think it would be as bad as it turned out." Boston players took runs at Park throughout the Stanley Cup finals and needled him from the bench. Still, Brad came out of it with honors. He was named to the First All-Star Team and was runner-up for the James Norris Trophy.

Park is to the Rangers what Bobby Orr is to the Bruins. Brad was fourth leading scorer for the New Yorkers, finishing the 1971-72 campaign with 24 goals and 49 assists for 73 points. These included eight power play goals and four game-winners. The genius of Park is recognized by the enemy everywhere, especially in Boston.

"When we play the Rangers," said Bruins manager Milt

Schmidt, "Park is the guy we have to handle just as Bobby Orr is the one they have to stop. Park is their Orr. He is vital in three areas—running the offense, working the power play from the point and killing penalties."

Brad was at his best in the third game of the Stanley Cup finals against Boston when he rifled two goals past Gerry Cheevers to power New York to a 5-2 victory. Cheevers' colleague, Ed Johnston, watched in awe from the bench as Brad's drives zipped into the twine.

"Park's two shots travelled so fast," said Johnston, "they smoked. Nobody stops that kind."

Aware of its potential, Brad has worked at perfecting his shot ever since he was a teenager. "I've always had a hard shot," he said, "but it was Gus Bodnar, my Junior coach, and my father who kept after me until I learned to keep in on the net and low. That's important because if your shot is blocked there's a chance of a rebound or a deflection."

Brad can fight as well as shoot. During the regular 1971-72 season he fought three Bruins and each time a second Boston skater was compelled to interrupt the match to rescue his teammate. As a result the Bruins came off with three game misconduct penalties because of Park.

Park has been battling ever since he startled everyone—except himself—by making the Ranger varsity in 1968-69. He startled a lot more people by grabbing off that First All-Star defense berth with Bobby Orr in the spring of 1970. And he startled absolutely no one by sharing the berth with Orr again at mid-season 1970-71.

It now has become apparent to professionals that Park not only is in Orr's class, but surpasses the Boston player in certain defensive skills.

"Park is a tremendous defenseman," said Ned Harkness, the Detroit Red Wings manager. "He moves the puck well, he rushed it, he's sound defensively. He's a great one. By comparison, Orr is more offensive-minded.

"But Brad is defensively sounder than Orr. Park turns well and is good around the net. When I saw the two of them paired together in the All-Star Game I said, boy, what a dream that is!"

It is a measure of Park's development as a professional that he is frequently being compared favorably with Orr.

Vancouver Canucks personnel director Hal Laycoe who, oddly enough, played for both Boston and New York, suggested that Park may outlast Orr because the Bruins defenseman is more susceptible to injury.

"Park is tough and aggressive," said Laycoe. "I'd say he's likely to have a longer and more productive career than Orr."

After watching Park deflate three Canadiens at the Montreal Forum, National Hockey League President Clarence Campbell said: "That kid looks like another Fern Flaman."

The development of Brad from peewee to professional is a case study in how parents *can* help their children. Park's father, Bob, and his mother, Betty, prudently but diligently advised their son once they realized he had special skating and stickhandling gifts.

"Brad started playing hockey when he was five," Mrs. Park recalled. "He couldn't see why he couldn't play if his older brother, who was three years older, already was in the game. Brad bugged his dad until finally they let him play goal. When they found out he could skate they put him up front."

Young hockey players often hone their skills to sharpness at the cost of a destructive household. In the Park home there were constant seismic reverberations as Brad pounced pucks off shingles, steps, and garage doors.

"By the time we moved to another home," said Mrs. Park, "there were more dents in the wood panelling than there were nails."

Both Bob and Betty Park kept their lines out to Brad as he moved up the hockey ladder. It was not unusual for Bob to be on the phone to Brad after an NHL game in his rookie year; always seeking to improve the boy. And Betty would get her lessons in, too.

"I'm very critical of him," she admitted. "If he doesn't hit within the first few minutes on the ice I don't think he's going to play the kind of game he's capable of playing. We always have felt that constructive criticism is helpful. Brad always needs an incentive." Needless to say, Bobby Orr has provided some of the best incentive available for Brad. A Toronto columnist remarked that had Orr arrived in another era, the praise for Park would even be more lavish.

"Bobby has had a definite influence on my play," said Park. "I began studying him in the 1968-69 season. While I was out with a broken ankle last year I saw him play twice on television and twice in person, not to mention the times I've seen him from the bench.

"One thing that impresses me is that he never panics. He slows play down and then, when he's drawn guys in, he'll bust out with his great skating speed."

Unlike Orr, Park is not surrounded by aggressive huskies. The Rangers remain a razzle-dazzle pass-the-puck team that will win by finesse rather than fuss. Ever since his rookie season Park has led the Rangers in bodychecking, a fact that surprised Francis, even in Brad's sophomore year. "The kid averaged seven hits a game in his second year, the same as he did in the first," said Francis. "At first I thought it was rookie luck or his strangeness to opposing forwards that was working for him. He became our top hitter by a wide margin."

It is quite possible that for the next decade critics and fans will be comparing Park to Orr, and vice versa. At the moment Orr is on top but this may not be a permanent state of affairs. And if it is, Brad will not mourn.

"I see no reason to be upset because I'm rated second to Bobby Orr," said Park. "Orr is not only the top defenseman in the game today, he is considered the best player ever to put on skates. What's wrong with being rated number two to such a super-super star? The fact that I am number two means that I'm considered better than all the other defensemen today, and there are some fine hockey players around."

Bobby Orr couldn't have said it better.

JEAN RATELLE Jean Ratelle was born 40 years too late. The beanpole New York Rangers center should have played hockey in 1932 with Frank Boucher and Bill Cook when it was a pure game and people didn't worry about images and business agents and hair stylists for men.

A French-Canadian who still speaks a bumpy brand of English, Ratelle belongs in another era, when ability mattered more than a mustache and finesse was king.

But 32-year-old Jean Ratelle is playing in the Seventies and ranks, perhaps, as the most unknown superstar in the National Hockey League. How else can one explain Ratelle's illogically low All-Star vote behind Boston's Phil Esposito although Ratelle led Esposito in first-half scoring?

The answer is that Ratelle, unlike Esposito, is not a contemporary man. He does not dress his hair; he does not dabble in a dozen businesses; he does not have a television program; and he militantly avoids the limelight. He is the arch anti-hero of the NHL.

"He's our straight-arrow," said teammate Brad Park. "Rat-ty is without a doubt the model hockey player; totally dedicated to the sport and the team. He plays hockey according to the rulebook and would never think of elbowing or smashing a guy or doing anything physical; he's just a beautiful player."

Which explains why in 1972 Ratelle won the Lady Byng Memorial Trophy as "the player adjudged to have exhibited the best type of sportsmanship and gentlemanly conduct combined with a high standard of playing ability." And why in 1971 he won the Bill Masterton Memorial Trophy as "the player who best exemplifies the qualities of perseverance, sportsmanship, and dedication to hockey."

It says nothing about ability but those with an Argus eye for talent spotted Ratelle's genius some time ago. "Jean is the guy who makes the Rangers go," said Boston goalie Gerry Cheevers before anyone else spotted Rat-ty. "He's New York's top forward."

That may have been true but it didn't show in the arithmetic until this year when Jean made it abundantly clear that he would wage a neck-and-neck battle for the Art Ross Trophy with Esposito. The 6-1, 175-pound Ranger was one point better than his Boston counterpart at mid-point but Esposito soon regained the lead and held it through February 9 although Jean was right behind with 33 goals and 53 assists for 86 points. Then a shot by teammate Dale Rolfe hit Jean in the ankle, sidelining him for the homestretch, until the Stanley Cup finals when a semi-crippled Ratelle vainly tried to rally the Rangers.

Inevitably, the question surfaces: who is the better player, Ratelle or Esposito? Phil is stronger and more goal-conscious. Jean is more artistic and diligent about playmaking. Esposito is more the virtuoso while Ratelle orchestrates the group behind the footlights.

Glen Sather, who played alongside Esposito in Boston and skated with Ratelle in Manhattan, put it another way: "Phil is more likely to try to overpower you while Jean finesses you."

Park put it another way: "Esposito is lucky there's a Bobby Orr on his team."

The point being that Ratelle, in conjunction with line-mates Rod Gilbert and Vic Hadfield, carried the Rangers last year—with some help from Park—while Esposito worked with the most talented team, man-for-man, in hockey.

Entering the last third of the season before Jean got hurt, the Ratelle line (also known as the "Gag"—goal-a-game—Line, or Hot Line) had accounted for about 45 percent of the Rangers' goals and 40 percent of the team's scoring points. An enemy coach didn't have to be Socrates to figure out that you trained your ack-ack on Ratelle and Company and forgot about the Ranger flubs. Result: Ratelle's bruises became more numerous and the Rangers became more ineffectual.

"There's definitely more pressure on us now that we are known," said Ratelle. "Other teams are concentrating more on checking us closely since they know we've been doing so well."

Thus, it is obvious that Jean was being noticeably underpaid at his estimated $60,000-a-year salary, especially in view of Esposito's $100,000-plus.

"It is pretty hard to compare yourself to a guy who has scored 76 goals," said Ratelle. "The most I had in a year—before last season—was 32. There's no comparison. But being close to Phil last season was a thrill to me. Before he retires he'll go down as one of the great centers of all time. I consider myself proven as a good center."

So good, in fact, that despite a severe ankle injury that sidelined him for the last 15 games of the 1971-72 season, Jean finished third in scoring behind Esposito and Bobby Orr with 46 goals and 63 assists for 109 points and only four minutes in penalties.

Playing with Hadfield and Gilbert for five consecutive years hasn't hurt. They became masters of the short-passing, puck-control game. Hadfield handled the heavy work while Gilbert and Ratelle did more of the dipsy-doodling.

Ratelle, who uses a flat-bladed stick, is one of the few remaining masters of the quick wrist shot and the back-handers.

"The fact that our line has been together so long means we have a pretty good idea where each guy is going to be on any given play," Ratelle explained. "I don't have to look; I just know Rod will be in such-and-such a place and, chances are, Vic will be where I think he'll be."

The sameness ends with their life-styles. Apart from being team captain, Hadfield is the team wit ("Just think, Jean," Vic once said, "if your nose keeps on growing across your face that way, it'll eventually be in your ear.") and Gilbert is the club sophisticate-bachelor, the supreme bird-watcher.

Ratelle's interests revolve around his family, his team, and the Dow Jones averages on the stock exchange. He expects to become a full-time broker when he retires and not long ago explained his market philosophy.

"Good investments, not speculative. . . . When the market was bad I sold some and put money in Canadian savings bonds. Now inflation is checked, the monetary situation seems solid and the economy good so the market will pick up."

He may be right, but there are a lot of wise men on Wall Street who only wish the market got as hot as Jean Ratelle's hockey stick.

WALT TKACZUK When Walt Tkaczuk emerged from the first two months of the 1971-72 season with only one goal despite regular turns and an occasional stint on the New York Rangers power play, his boss, Emile Francis, yawned with militant non-concern.

"I'm not worried about Walter," said Francis. "He's a hard worker who never lets up. Sooner or later the goals will come for him."

Since Tkaczuk turned pro with the Rangers in 1968 he has only done one thing to annoy Francis and that is hold out for more money in a contract dispute in the fall of 1970. Other than that he has been, as Francis puts it, "a great young hockey player."

In 76 games last season, Tkaczuk scored 24 goals and 42 assists for 66 points. Compared with Boston's Phil Esposito, Tkaczuk appears almost miserly in his production but Walter does things defensively that Esposito has yet to learn and Tkaczuk, according to teammates and foes alike, is virtually indestructible and unstoppable when he develops a head of steam for a rush down the ice. Walter's toughness is, in a sense, hereditary. His father, Mike, was a driller for the Jamieson Copper Mine in South Porcupine, Ontario. For a short time, young Walter worked as a $1.80-an-hour employee in the nearby gold mines.

"I was a pipe-fitter," said Walter. "That was in the first summer. The year after that I worked deep in the mine, about 3,300 feet down. My job was to go into the holes alongside the little railroad and follow the vein of gold. I walked on rock all the time."

The dangerous part of the job was in Tkaczuk's hands. He carried sticks of dynamite and an air drill to separate the gold from the rock.

"We'd plant the dynamite and light the fuse and then get away from there. If you used ten sticks of dynamite you had to listen for 10 blasts. I remember one time we planted five sticks but there were only four blasts. But two had gone off together."

Walter escaped the mines without any serious injury and began his hockey in earnest with the Kitchener Rangers of the Ontario Hockey Association's Junior A League. In April 1968 he won the Albert "Red" Tilson Memorial Award as the league's most valuable player, beating out Tom Webster now with the California Golden Seals and Danny Lawson of the Buffalo Sabres.

"Tkaczuk stood out," said New York scout Steve Brklacich. "He went where the puck was, fought for it and when he had it, he was a hard man to knock off it."

Walter scored a modest 12 goals and 24 assists for 36 points in his NHL rookie year (1968-69) but he lifted his total to 27-50-77 in 76 games the following season. By that time he had impressed Francis with his bulldozer qualities.

"He doesn't take the overland route," said Francis. "The overland route is trying to go around somebody. Walter stays on a straight line. I remember in his first season when he was coming in on Bobby Baun, one of the toughest checkers in the league, and I thought, 'Oh, no, Walter.'

"But he kept going right at him and knocked Baun back ten feet, and kept going toward the net. That's the kind of strength he has. When he goes into a corner for the puck with two or three guys, he not only comes out with it most of the time, but he's not even off balance. He's a strong kid."

To Francis' dismay, Tkaczuk also was strong in his contract demands during the late summer and early fall of 1970. Aligned with teammates Brad Park, Vic Hadfield, and Jean Ratelle, Walter defied Francis to the point of even missing the first two games of the regular season before he finally signed a contract estimated at the time as $35,000.

"I served my apprenticeship," said Tkaczuk. "Two years. Now this is the biggest salary increase I can ever hope for. After a few more good years, I wouldn't get it in one big jump anymore. This is my only chance to make it."

He made it big on the contract and then made it big on

the ice, leading the Rangers to their best season in years and reinforcing the words of Rangers' scout Lou Passador who said of Tkaczuk: "He's a hell of a guy. Just all business—and strong!"

But the Tkaczuk that people such as Passador had touted didn't really emerge until the 1972 Stanley Cup playoffs. Barreling past the enemy like a heavy tank through grass, Tkaczuk was the essential reason why the Rangers were able to dispatch Montreal and Chicago to the sidelines in the quarter and semifinals, respectively.

When the Rangers finally confronted the Bruins in the Stanley Cup finals it was Tkaczuk who thoroughly blanketed, shut out, and overshadowed league-leading scorer Phil Esposito. "I've never run into anyone tougher, ever," said Esposito. "Bobby Clarke of Philadelphia gives me fits because he's so fast and persistent. Jim Harrison in Toronto was as strong as a horse but Tkaczuk had a combination of those qualities."

It is Tkaczuk's hope—and the Rangers' belief—that the best of Walter will be displayed during the 1972-73 season and, as a result, the New Yorkers will finish in first place for the first time in 31 years.

MIKE WALTON It was the second game of the 1972 Stanley Cup finals between the Boston Bruins and the New York Rangers. The score was tied, 1-1, in the third period as 14,995 fans in Boston Garden nervously wondered whether their favorites would be able to make the break that would win the hockey game.

Then it happened. Two successive penalties gave Boston a 5-3 advantage in skaters and a chance for the Bruins' super power play. The puck slithered to Mike "Shaky" Walton along the left boards. He moved forward toward the New York net, spotting big Ken Hodge standing in front of Rangers goalie Gilles Villemure.

"I was trying to back up to create some interference,"

said Hodge, "while Mike had room to come in closer. But he made a good play. He had his head up and saw that I was open and he put the puck on my stick."

The rest is history. Hodge flipped the puck past Villemure to give Boston the winning goal in a decisive 2-1 victory that eventually led to Boston's Stanley Cup. But the unsung hero in the episode was Walton, a complex young man who not very long ago appeared at the end of his rope as a hockey player. A vignette that unfolded less than two years ago tells the story about Walton's battle with himself and against certain enemies in hockey. There was Mike Walton. There were a pair of skis and there was snow on the ground.

He didn't appear disturbed, the way everyone said he had been.

The striped woolen ski cap gripped snugly over his ears and his eyes were bright and gay as he lifted the black metal skis off his automobile roof and carried them into his home in Toronto. Michael Robert Walton appeared to be the very soul of contentment. On the surface.

But underneath, this very gifted 28-year-old forward was suffering a bubbling metabolism on that afternoon of January 31, 1971. For more than a month he had been tortured with a problem that rarely afflicts an athlete but when it does, his abilities descend to the zero point of no return.

Mike Walton, professional hockey player, was psychologically unable to play hockey anymore for his team, the Toronto Maple Leafs. Quite simply, a psychiatrist had warned the Leafs—trade this player, or else!

Later that night Mike's depression was finally to be lifted. The Maple Leafs accepted the doctor's advice and on the evening of January 31 Walton was bounced in a three-cornered trade from Toronto to Philadelphia and, ultimately, Boston, where he became a surprise asset to the big bad Bruins. Last season he scored 28 goals and 28 assists for 56 points. This was surprising when one considers his previous problems, and the solution. The result was a rarity in sports, and one that was to have wide-spread repercussions in years to come. The Walton psychiatrist episode was to play a major part in getting Alex Johnson of the California Angels a favorable decision in his battle with the baseball team. Like Walton, Johnson was suffering from an emotional disturbance. But first let's examine Mike's fascinating case—from stardom to the couch and back to stardom again.

The son of a minor league hockey ace, Bob "Shaky" Walton, Mike was raised in the Maple Leaf minor hockey organization during the Punch Imlach dynasty. Imlach ruled the Leafs the way Mao ruled China. He brooked no nonsense and loathed talented scorers—like Walton— who, according to Imlach, failed to attend to defensive chores as well.

Nevertheless, Walton became a full-fledged Leaf in 1966-67 and promptly rode the bench. When Imlach finally gave Mike a starting assignment he scored a three-goal "hat trick." It was the beginning of Walton's brief happiness days in Toronto. The goals came easy and the praise followed like foam with an onrushing wave.

"Mike looks like an angry water spider," said ex-NHL goalie Charlie Hodge. "With him, the strange thing is that you don't notice the guy til he gets the puck. His moves are amazing."

But soon the sun stopped shining for Walton. Imlach disapproved of his all-offense, no-defense style and clashes between the two became more and more evident. On top of that Mike was related to the Smythe family through marriage. Conn Smythe, the patriarch, was a founder and president of the Maple Leafs. The late Stafford Smythe, Conn's son and acid-tongued successor, was the Leafs' president while Mike was a Leaf player. The fact that Walton was married to Candy Hoult, Conn's granddaughter and Stafford's niece, made life complicated for Mike.

Playing for Punch made it that much more burdensome until, finally, it happened: he couldn't take Imlach anymore.

One day in February 1969, Walton walked out on the Maple Leafs. Just plain quit the team in mid-season during a hectic run for the playoffs. Obviously Mike didn't want to play for Punch, and wouldn't, until a meeting between club officials, Walton's attorney, and close friend Al Eagleson, and senior Leaf players finally brought about Walton's return; but not an end to his troubles.

The Leafs faced Boston in the opening 1969 Stanley Cup playoff round and were demolished like no Toronto playoff team ever was demolished in Cup competition.

Boston won in four straight games and Imlach was fired on the spot after the final humiliation of fourth-game defeat.

If Imlach's departure was the tonic to restore Walton's thirst for hockey he didn't betray that attitude to the public. Under rookie coach John McLellan, Walton played spotty hockey: electrifyingly superb one night and muddily disinterested on three other evenings of skating. Obviously the problem wasn't Imlach and it wasn't McLellan; but it was the stifling hockey atmosphere of Toronto.

"What bugged me," said quick-talking, long-haired Mike, "was that in Toronto I'd come through but I still had to keep proving myself.

"It wasn't that way with other players. One season Dave Keon scored only 11 goals with the Leafs but he was never benched. Another year Norm Ullman scored 18 goals and played all the time. But I put a 30-goal season (1967-68) together and followed that with 22 goals the next year and was leading the team a season later before injuries put me on the shelf. That wasn't bad hockey. But when I showed up at camp last year I wound up as swing third-line center with Jim Harrison."

If those are not the ingredients that would drive a proud stickhandler to distraction, Mike would like to know just what would. He was scoring for a team that needed goals. He was consistent, at least in *his* eyes, and he was outscoring his competitors, particularly Harrison. Mike has insisted all along that he had no beef with Harrison, Keon, and Ullman; all fine fellows. He just wanted to play.

"I'm only trying to explain why things were always driving me nuts," said Mike. "I never got the feeling I belonged."

This gnawing feeling of insecurity heightened within Mike as the 1970-71 season began. By late November he was terribly depressed. Toronto won a game, 7-2, but Mike looked on helplessly from the bench, hardly ever participating in the rout. Despondent to the core, he left Maple Leaf Gardens after the game and phoned his pal, Al Eagleson.

Mike spilled his woes out and Al got moving. Eagleson, an honest and often outspoken executive director of the NHL Players' Association, conferred with Maple Leaf manager Jim Gregory and Dr. Hugh Smythe, brother of the late Stafford Smythe. The team physician, Dr. Smythe addressed himself to Walton's ice deportment, not Mike's mental state. At least, that's Eagleson's story.

"To my astonishment," said Eagleson, "and with me sitting there, Dr. Smythe told him what bad hockey he'd been playing. 'You don't pass the puck enough,' he told Mike. I mean, what the hell, he's only the bloody doctor."

By this time Walton wanted no part of the Toronto hockey club nor Maple Leaf Gardens. When coach McLellan next called a practice Mike failed to show up and manager Gregory promptly suspended him—without pay. Eagleson realized that his client—not to mention his buddy—needed help. He dispatched Walton to a psychiatrist who reported that Mike was significantly depressed. Eagleson then required NHL President Clarence Campbell to lift Walton's suspension.

Campbell balked and, instead of complying, selected an NHL-sanctioned psychiatrist to examine Mike. Dr. Ronald Stokes of Toronto's Clarke Institute of Psychiatry was the man. Walton submitted to an examination after which the following report was filed:

"It is my opinion that this man is currently suffering from a depressive illness which will be aggravated, and I believe to serious proportions, if he were to continue to play hockey for this particular organization (the Leafs).

"There is longstanding ill will and conflict with this organization that is substantially aggravated through his family relationship." The substance was that Walton should get as far away from the Toronto team as possible. The late Stafford Smythe's reaction was surprisingly understanding.

"I agree with the doctor," Smythe said. "I just don't know how things would have turned out with me if I hadn't been able to get away for four years during the war. That gave me a chance to assess the situation from a distance and adapt to it. I never would have followed my father into hockey if I hadn't had that period out of Toronto.

"I grew up with the same extreme family pressure all my life and I know what it's like. It's tough. I can guess how Mike feels."

The center of the controversy, Walton, called a press

conference and frankly aired his views. He made it clear that, although Toronto hockey wasn't his cup of ice, he *did* want to continue in the NHL. Anywhere. That is, anywhere but Toronto or Buffalo under Imlach. "I certainly want to play," he said. "I think it might be the best remedy for me."

Toronto opened trade negotiations with several teams but failed to conclude a deal until January 31. In the three-cornered trade Mike and goalie Bruce Gamble were dispatched to Philadelphia for goalie Bernie Parent. Walton, in turn, was sent to Boston for Rick MacLeish and Dan Schock.

(The use of the league-appointed psychiatrist to help Walton later came to the attention of Marvin Miller, executive director of the Major League Baseball Players' Association. When Alex Johnson encountered problems in California, Miller obtained evidence in the Walton case and submitted it in behalf of the beleaguered Johnson. Miller asserts that the Walton file helped obtain a favorable decision for Johnson.)

There was little doubt that the trade lifted the gray pall over Walton's psyche the moment he walked into Boston Garden early in February 1971. He was greeted by center Derek Sanderson, wearing an outrageous Edwardian suit, and Phil Esposito, adorned with a black turtle neck and yellow cardigan. It was a remarkable contrast to the severe sartorial regulations of Maple Leaf Gardens where players were forbidden to enter without shirt and tie.

"The Bruins," said a suddenly exuberant Walton, "are my kind of team."

What he meant was that his new teammates exhibited a brand of loosey-goosey behavior that just wasn't part of the conservative Maple Leaf genre and the suddenly extroverted Mike promptly jumped on the bandwagon. On one of his first roadtrips with his new club the Bruins were stranded in O'Hare Airport, Chicago. Mike laid his valise horizontal on the floor of the O'Hare waiting room and casually stretched out on it, knowing full well that it suggested to all viewers a psychiatrist's couch.

His teammates were vastly amused and one of them shouted, "Hey, Mike, was it like this with the Leafs?"

"No way. You guys are all crazy. I've never been with a team like this."

Although Mike was used sparingly—he had been out of condition—by the Bruins late in the 1970-71 season he did lift his new club during the East Division playoff with Montreal, scoring two goals and successfully taking on the Canadiens' policeman John Ferguson in a couple of fights. But the Bruins' sudden elimination from the 1971 Cup round dimmed the lustre of Walton's performance, not to mention his comeback from the psychiatrist's couch. The relevant question in September 1971 was how would Mike Walton fit in with the 1971-72 Bruins? The answer was supplied quickly and emphatically in training camp. Very well, thank you, very well. And it was underlined as he helped Boston win the Stanley Cup.

LORNE "GUMP" WORSLEY Fat and fortyish, Lorne "Gump" Worsley suggests a skating dirigible when he takes the ice for Minnesota's North Stars; a less likely looking athlete there never has been, in or out of the National Hockey League. Yet, last season he played so superbly at age 42 that one critic described Worsley as the best goaltender anywhere.

Certainly his 1971-72 record bespeaks competence. Playing in 34 games, Worsley allowed only 68 goals for a sparkling 2.12 average. Not only that, but he appeared to be leading the North Stars to a Stanley Cup first-round victory over the St. Louis Blues when enemy defenseman Bob Plager bashed The Gump into the net, knocking him clear out of the series. It was no coincidence that once Worsley was gone from the Minnesota lineup the North Stars were finished as Cup contenders.

A 5-7, 180-pounder when he's in top condition, Worsley is amazing for more reasons than his pot belly, or his age. He remains the only veteran goaltender in the NHL who still refuses to wear a protective face mask.

"I tried one once," Worsley recalled. "It was with the Rangers and I put the mask on during practice. Next thing

I knew I got hit with a puck; the mask cracked, cut me up, and I decided then and there I'd do without one. I'm too old to start worrying about things like that."

There are times when Worsley plays so spectacularly, friend and foe alike stare in disbelief. One such occasion was the night of February 7, 1971, when The Gump disrupted the spectacular Boston Bruins scoring machine in a hostile rink. Following his performance, Worsley, an exhausted butterball of a man, leaned back on his bench in the bowels of Boston Garden and smiled. "The way I played tonight," said Worsley, "I must have made the oldtimers feel good."

The then 41-year-old Worsley, ancient by National Hockey League standards, had just made 63 saves against the Bruins to provide Minnesota with a tie. The North Stars should have been defeated.

"I've never seen a better job of goaltending by anyone," said Bruins goalie Ed Johnston. "I certainly haven't seen Gump play a better game."

Worsley was a prime reason why the North Stars were able to reach the Stanley Cup semifinals before bowing in six games to the world champion Montreal Canadiens.

A throwback to an earlier hockey era, Worsley has no illusions about his ability to play a 70-game season, the way he did in 1955-56 for the New York Rangers. "A goalie can't go the entire route these days," said Worsley. "The schedule is too long and the puck is coming at you too fast. You show me a goalie who plays every game and I'll show you a guy who'll be swinging from a tree by the time the season's over."

It was over a decade ago that Worsley realized fully the dangers of goaltending. In December 1960 a shot ricocheted off a stick like a bullet hitting a rock and struck Gump in the left eye. He was taken to the dressing room where the doctor told him he was lucky. He was cut above and below the eye but he wasn't blinded; at least not permanently.

His manager, Muzz Patrick, asked Gump if he could continue. Worsley nodded. He had a 2-0 lead in the first period. When the game had ended he had a 5-2 lead. But he didn't see out of the left eye until a day later.

"Going back on the ice was the craziest thing I've ever done," Worsley said later. Then he paused and grinned that impish grin of his and added, "But you've got to be crazy to be a goalie."

For ten more years the man who looks like a bloated fire hydrant blocked National Hockey League shots. In time he was traded from New York to his native Montreal. Playing for the Canadiens, he helped the Flying Frenchmen to a few Stanley Cups and clearly established himself as one of the supreme—if not most unlikely-looking—goaltenders big-league hockey has known. He loved being a hero in his own home town.

"When I retire," he said, "it'll be because I can't help this club anymore."

Not long after that the Canadiens and Gump began feuding and soon Montreal manager Sam Pollock opened negotiations with Wren Blair of Minnesota to deal Gump to the North Stars. If Worsley was angry at Pollock for prior treatment he received, he was even more furious over the manner in which he learned he was traded to the North Stars. He heard about it on the radio.

Heading for the North Stars in February 1970 was like being sent on a rescue boat to help the *Titanic*. Minnesota was sinking in the quicksand of an endless losing streak that threatened to shut the club out of the playoffs. Optimism was nonexistent.

The desperate Minnesotans looked to Worsley to save them. Somehow, somewhere, he was quoted as saying, he'd lead them to the holy grail. It was not quite accurate. "I didn't say I'd make sure Minnesota would be in the playoffs," Worsley remembered. "I was misquoted. I said I'd do everything possible to help them make it."

North Star coach Charlie Burns made it clear he didn't expect any miracles from Worsley. "He told me to go into the dressing room and say what I wanted to say. They hadn't won in so long that nobody wanted the puck. They'd come off the bench and sit there like wooden Indians. The first thing I did was talk to them. Next thing I knew they went up against Toronto and won, 8-0. I was on the bench and every time it got quiet I'd get up and start cheering and yelling. They never had a guy like that before.

"When they were down a goal they'd get upset. I told them that in the NHL if you're down a goal you've got lots of time to get it back. All of a sudden we started to win. But what surprised me was that after only two practices they asked me to play."

On Saturday night, March 14, 1970, Worsley was in the nets, beating Pittsburgh. On Sunday, Burns asked him to play again, this time in Madison Square Garden against New York. It was a difficult request because Worsley did not care for back-to-back assignments at his age. "Charlie asked me to play as long as I could," Gump said. "I figured I'd give it a try."

It was a memorable effort. The Gump exploited every resource at his command, both mental and physical. Overwhelmed by the onrushing Rangers, the North Stars nevertheless held fast as Worsley blunted the New York attack. A goal by Ray Cullen late in the game put Minnesota ahead.

If the often-cynical Gump calls it "one of the better games in my career," it had to have been an NHL classic. More important to the North Stars, it gave them the momentum to challenge the faltering Philadelphia Flyers for a playoff berth. On Saturday afternoon, April 4, the Flyers played their final home game of the season. All they needed was a tie against the North Stars—as it turned out, all they needed was a goal—to win a playoff berth.

Gump Worsley did not allow the Flyers one goal. At 7:48 of the third period, defenseman Barry Gibbs of the North Stars lifted a Texas League shot into the Philadelphia end of the rink. It was the kind of shot that amateur goalies are supposed to stop but it bounced past Bernie Parent and the Flyers lost the game, 1-0.

"That's hockey," explained Worsley. "This game is strange. Things happen that you can't believe."

Take Gump Worsley as an example.

THE OTHER HOCKEYS

THE BIRTH OF STREET HOCKEY

BY MIKE RUBIN
President, Columbia University Street Hockey Club

WHEN the Boston Bruins reached the playoffs, finishing third in 1968, the city of Boston adopted hockey as its favorite pastime. Before long, suburban communities surrounding Boston formed high school, neighborhood, and various other amateur ice hockey leagues, so that kids would have an opportunity to play in organized games.

When school and the hockey season began in the fall of 1968, I was 15 years old and entering my junior year of high school in Newton, a city just west of Boston. At the time, it was difficult finding a suitable place to play ice hockey, since local rinks were packed to capacity. Besides, none of us could really skate well enough to satisfy our "Walter Mitty" fantasies of playing on the Bruins.

One November day, I was walking home after school when I saw what appeared to be a hockey game going on in the school's parking lot! It seemed hard to believe, but as I moved closer, I noticed that these kids were indeed playing hockey—with some major modifications. Instead of gliding on skates, the players were all running around on shoes or sneakers. Also, a tennis ball was used in place of a hockey puck, and the goals were simple cardboard boxes. Instead of having six men to a side as in ice hockey, there were only two forwards, one defenseman, and one goalie to a team. The only unmodified pieces of equipment were the sticks, although most of the blades were badly worn.

I was fascinated by the simplicity of the game. There were no "off-sides" or "icing" calls to worry about; action would cease only if the ball was shot out of bounds. Also, the risk of injury was extremely low, since there were no sharp-edged pucks or skates. As soon as the game was over, I spoke with a few of the players. They told me they had been playing this game called "street hockey" for a couple of months, and were lacking only competition. Apparently there were no more than two or three teams in existence.

I went right home, discussed the great new idea with my brother, Rick, and then we immediately began a search for interested players. As it turned out, five of my friends were very enthusiastic about the idea, so the seven of us formed one of the area's first organized street hockey teams.

When we finally felt ready to play an "official" game, I contacted another new team and arranged a match on a Sunday afternoon. The outcome of the game was a tribute to our ten weeks of practice: we won, 6-4. After that, I believe we got a little cocky, because we challenged the best team in the city. This team called themselves the "Mad Dogs" and their name described their style of play. I wouldn't say that they played dirty; "overzealous" is the proper term. In any case they put us in our place, 25-3!

There was one problem with street hockey that required immediate attention: some of the equipment we had been using was definitely unsatisfactory. Our problem was the poor quality of the sticks. The ordinary wooden hockey sticks we used wore down very quickly on the asphalt surface. I used to buy a new stick every three weeks. I really couldn't afford such extravagance for long, so I tried attaching various protective materials to the bottom of my stick, but they always came loose.

Another problem was the fragility of our cardboard-box goals. Not only were they too small, but they were usually accidentally squashed in the course of a game. However, we were unsuccessful in our attempts to find a suitable replacement.

The last piece of equipment that gave us trouble was the tennis ball. We had hoped that it would simulate a hockey puck, but it bounced around too much to be realistic. We even tried wrapping tennis balls in hockey tape to decrease the bounce. That only succeeded in making the balls too big and heavy. Besides, the tape would peel off early in the game.

We began our second season in the autumn of 1969

fully aware of these problems, but unable to find satisfactory solutions. By this time street hockey teams had formed all over the Greater Boston area, so we temporarily forgot about equipment troubles and concentrated on setting up intercity play. I figured that if my team was going to play against rough competition from other cities, I had better acquire some additional manpower. I spoke with Steve Sacks, a good friend of mine and captain of a rival team, about a possible "merger" between our two teams. Steve liked the idea; we merged and called ourselves the "Newton South Stars," the name of Steve's former team.

Now we were ready for intercity play. I contacted Don Rocci, the player-coach of a team from Jamaica Plain (a section of Boston), and we arranged what I believe was the first intercity street hockey match ever. Don and I decided that if the first game was a success, we would initiate a continuous home-and-home series—that is, we would take turns playing in Newton and Jamaica Plain for the rest of the season. A coin toss decided that the first game would be played in Newton.

It turned out, naturally, that the members of the Jamaica Plain team were just as apprehensive as we were before the game. We were a little more psyched up than they were, though, because we beat them 7-6, thanks to a hat trick by Gary Rubenstein, one of our top forwards.

Next, we immediately set a date for the return match in Jamaica Plain. We were pleasantly surprised by the friendly atmosphere, and our even friendlier hosts beat us 4-1. We then played against Jamaica Plain once every two or three weeks until the end of the season. We also scheduled some other games with local teams, and when the season ended in June of 1970, we had played a total of fourteen games, winning six and losing eight.

After the Boston Bruins beat the St. Louis Blues to win the Stanley Cup in May 1970, enthusiasm for street hockey reached its highest point ever with at least 10,000 kids in Greater Boston playing the game. Teams were organized all over eastern Massachusetts, and it was clear that a league would have to be created to permit at least some of the teams to play on a regular basis.

The first step in the formation of such an organization was taken by John Bannusiewicz, a junior at Lynn Classical High School. (Lynn is a city to the north of Boston.) John contacted teams from cities in the Greater Boston area, including Newton and Jamaica Plain, and formed the Greater Boston Street Hockey League, with two five-team divisions.

The impact of the Greater Boston Street Hockey League was tremendous. Not only did the stickhandlers appreciate the excitement and realism of league play, but there were also many businessmen who helped by sponsoring teams. They provided jerseys and equipment in return for advertising on the backs of uniforms.

But the most important development was the creation of companies to manufacture special street hockey equipment. In the summer of 1970, Mylec Inc. started making a special hockey stick with a tough plastic blade that could be used on any surface suitable for street hockey.

Soon thereafter, companies such as Cooper, Franklin, and Rally followed Mylec's lead, and they developed other important pieces of equipment. One of these items is a "street hockey ball" to be used in place of tennis balls or hockey pucks. The ball is bright orange and approximately the size and weight of a tennis ball, but made of tough, yet soft plastic, instead of rubber. Because of its consistency, the street hockey ball will not bounce. It will remain on the ground while in play, unlike a tennis ball, which usually has to be batted out of the air. With the appearance of this unique ball, a new kind of realism was added to street hockey.

The third major piece of equipment was a street hockey goal. Made of aluminum piping and a nylon net stretched over the back of the goal and tied to the goalposts, the net measures approximately 3½' x 4½' between the posts and about 1¼' deep. This is considerably smaller than regulation NHL goals (6' x 4'), but perfect for street hockey. The goal even folds up for easy storage.

One of the men developing street hockey equipment is Phil Esposito, All-Star center for the Boston Bruins, who vividly remembers playing street hockey himself as a youngster in Sault Ste. Marie, Ontario.

"When I was a kid," says Phil, "brother Tony and I couldn't wait all year for the ice to freeze. We played hockey anytime and anywhere . . . in driveways, parking lots, and in the streets. We had no equipment and had to make our own. First, we would take a tennis ball and punch it full of nail holes so that it wouldn't bounce too much. Even with all these holes, it still bounced a lot, so we had to find an old piece of plywood and nail it to the blades of our sticks so that the ball wouldn't hop over the blade.

"For goals, we used two-by-fours and chicken wire. . . . We had a goal of sorts, but it was always lopsided. Our goalie—usually Tony—would use an old broom and baseball glove for equipment. None of this equipment would last very long; our sticks wore out so fast on the hardtop they looked like toothpicks, and we spent almost as much time repairing them as we did playing. It's been a long way from Sault Ste. Marie to the Boston Bruins, but I've never forgotten those early days."

In the fall of 1970, I came to New York City to attend Columbia University, and launched street hockey in Manhattan with the help of a friend, Dave Wolinsky. Working together, we managed to find five other people who wanted to try street hockey. One of them, Mike Trott, had actually played a form of street hockey earlier at his home on Long Island, New York. The rest were totally inexperienced.

We began playing "official" games in February of 1971, and by April, the Columbia Street Hockey Club boasted twenty-five members. We played four more games that year and then called it quits for vacation.

During the summer, the National Street Hockey Association, an organization based in Boston, was founded to integrate the various leagues throughout the state, and perhaps even the country. The Association now plans annual tournaments in addition to other street hockey events.

When I returned to Columbia for my sophomore year, we picked up where we had left off. Our roster expanded to 35 players and continues to grow. We conduct street hockey "clinics," introducing the special hockey equipment, and we are confident that once the equipment is made available to city kids street hockey will grow throughout the continent, just as it has in Boston and many other NHL cities. If we can get people to recognize street hockey as a safe, simple, and exciting game, all our work will have been worthwhile.

ROLLER HOCKEY

WHILE Canadians have been boasting—and with good reason—that ice hockey is Canada's invention and national pastime, they have overlooked the fact that Americans invented a similar game called roller hockey. As the name implies it is played on roller skates, and even if it is not "the national pastime" it's popularity is widespread.

Many Canadians are rather surprised to learn about roller hockey's close development with the ice counterpart and they are further astonished when they learn of the zeal with which it is played and the hardships involved.

I speak from experience. My introduction to the game was in 1938, at the age of six, on an exceedingly rough sidewalk in Queens, New York City. In due time I graduated to the streets of Brooklyn and reached my pinnacle as a third-string defenseman on the Woodside Whippets, a team which finished second in the Long Island City YMCA League (1946-47).

Unfortunately, my involvement with the game never enabled me to determine its exact roots. I am told by unofficial roller hockey savants that crude versions of the sport date back to the 1800s when skates were nothing more than empty thread-spools roughly attached to shoes.

Roller hockey, as we know it today, really took hold in New York City late in the 1930s at the same time that the New York Rangers were at or near the top of the NHL. Naturally, the game took on many forms.

In its most primitive state roller hockey could be played with anywhere from two to six men on a team. The puck often was nothing more than the end of a wooden cottage cheese container and shin pads were unheard of—which is why the venerable cry *"DON'T LIFT THE PUCK!"* came into existence.

In the early days of World War II there were few autos on the New York streets—gas rationing took care of that—so it was quite common for roller hockey to become a "gutter game." The curbs made a natural boundary and the goals consisted of sewer-covers with, perhaps, an extension on each side drawn in chalk.

"Gutter hockey" had its amusing overtones. In the Flatbush area of Brooklyn, for example, one team developed a knack of having its forwards latch on to the rear of passing trucks. This enabled them to gain great momentum when the vehicle passed. They then would release themselves, capture the puck, and whirl in on the opposition goalie before the defense could move.

Another version of the game was practiced in some especially tough neighborhoods when I played in the Long Island City, Queens, League. The home team would fortify its cheering section with a large contingent of "big guys." When a visiting player would be knocked onto the sidewalk he would be "helped" to his feet by several of these spectators but, somehow, would find himself moderately bruised about the head by the time he got back into the play.

Since the New York City Engineering Bureau never laid out its streets with roller hockey dimensions in mind, several middle-of-the-avenue rinks were improperly balanced. The Sunnyside, Queens, Americans, for example, played on a court that seemed to have a ski slope pitch. Very wisely, the Americans skated downhill for two out of the three periods. I vividly recall a game in which the Whippets led the Americans, 6-2, in the third period. With ten minutes remaining the Whippets were skating uphill more like tortoises. The Americans scored three quick goals and, I recall, we crowded around our goal net, victims of an avalanche. Our great captain, Jim Hernon, cleared the puck out of danger just when it appeared that Whippets, net, and goalie would be swept down the hill into the subway station.

By this time some insightful player discovered that a medium-sized roll of black tape duplicated the action of a regular ice-hockey puck and tape became the official puck of the game. Unsolved, however, were such problems as how to keep dungarees from ripping at the knee after sliding on macadam to block a shot and how to prevent skates from falling off in the middle of a breakaway.

The skate problem was remedied in the fifties when

steel wheels were affixed to traditional indoor rink skates. The ripped dungaree dilemma remains.

As one might expect, roller hockey hotbeds emerged throughout the city. One of them sprouted in the vicinity, if not the shadows, of the old Madison Square Garden. There were others in such areas of New York City as Chelsea, Jackson Heights, Elmhurst, Bensonhurst, Bay Ridge, and Borough Park.

One roller hockey team, the Williamsburgh Wizards, created their own hotbed when they couldn't find competition in their neighborhood during the early fifties. Several players attended a vocational high school and constructed portable nets which could be quickly assembled and disassembled. Thus, the Wizards would carry the net parts on top of two autos (passengers were required to keep windows open so that they could hold down the parts with their hands) and drive five miles to Park Slope where they would reconstruct the nets and play their games in a schoolyard also used by several other teams. They then would pack up again, hold the nets on top of the car, and drive home. During midwinter, the Wizards lost more games to frostbite than to opponents.

Roller hockey progress came slow in some communities. A team from Greenpoint, Brooklyn, insisted on playing the game *without* skates on the grounds that it was eminently more sensible than using the contraptions that kept falling off your shoes. Lack of opponents forced it out of action, just as it did another Williamsburgh team which played on a slope but which insisted the opponents had to skate uphill for *three* periods.

Unlike their professional counterparts in the NHL, roller hockey players didn't always travel first-class. The Woodside Whippets resorted to bus lines for their more distant away games although they often talked their way off the bus. It was not uncommon for a team wag to shout from the rear of the vehicle, "Does your father work?" Whereupon a teammate would respond, "No, he's a bus driver!" At least once, the Whippets were ordered off the bus following the punchline.

For less distant trips, the players simply strapped on their skates and rolled their way across the city streets until they found the enemy rink. Thus, on a Saturday afternoon in Jackson Heights or Woodside in Queens or

Manhattan's Upper West Side, a normal sight is a flock of young skaters dodging through traffic, their sticks over their shoulders and their little equipment bags hung through the stick blades enroute to the contest.

During the late forties it became the goal of several players to find an indoor roller rink where games could be played in more professional surroundings. For a short time a fast indoor version of the sport flourished at the Eastern Parkway Roller Rink in Brooklyn and some rinks in New Jersey. There were great hopes for establishing a professional league with television coverage and similar big-league trappings. The idea did get off the ground but lack of available rinks and players, not to mention competition from other sports, scuttled the plan.

Always, for the roller hockey player, there was the lure of ice. Unfortunately, a dearth of ice rinks which permit hockey has always been New York's problem. During the late forties and fifties, the Brooklyn Ice Palace hosted hockey late on Friday and Saturday nights, following the regular skating sessions. Occasionally, a roller hockey team would make the transition to ice, as was the case with the Park Slope Rangers. But the Ice Palace was soon closed and the troops returned to roller skates.

Still, the roller hockey experience proved invaluable to the boys who made the transition. One who did it better than most was Sal Messina, an Astoria roller hockey goalie who got as far as a New York Ranger tryout and who now is a minor official at Madison Square Garden NHL games. Ed Bjorness and Norm Diviney, who learned their roller hockey in Bay Ridge, Brooklyn, graduated to the Quebec Junior Hockey League in the forties and at one time were regarded as professional prospects.

Unfortunately roller hockey never achieved the organization or stature of its ice counterpart. As a result some of the game's truly extraordinary stars remain eulogized only by their neighborhood cronies. In Jackson Heights, they'll tell you that little Ronnie Messenger of the Elmwood Capitols was the Bobby Orr of his time and that Jim Hernon was the Gordie Howe.

Those who played against a goalie named Frank Pagello—who liked to smoke a cigarette during the action—of the Park Slope Rangers would have been the equal of Ed Giacomin if he had grown up in Northern Ontario instead of South Brooklyn. Bert Korwin, who still plays every Sunday in Bayside, had every one of Gordie Howe's assets including his elbows but he's a department store manager instead of an NHL star. Mike Cleary is now considered the Vic Hadfield of Brooklyn roller hockey.

Then, as now some of the boys took the game terribly seriously and hoped against hope that someday, somehow they would make it to the NHL. Most, however, played hard but realized that roller hockey was nothing more than a fun neighborhood game to be played with a loosey-goosey attitude.

The Brooklyn Wizards epitomized this philosophy. In 1950-51 they defeated the Flatbush Ramblers in a playoff series and felt a great need to honor themselves. They decided they had won the Inter-Park Championship and then all 12 Wizards went out and bought themselves a dozen trophies.

SPECIAL BONUS SECTION

THE MOD STICKHANDLER

"THERE were a lot of good guys in St. Louis," Gene Carr, the New York Rangers young forward, was saying, "but there were the old guys and the new guys. They bothered me about my hair, about living with Unger. They said I was trying to copy him."

The Unger they said he wanted to copy was the Garry Unger whom Ned Harkness had dealt from Detroit in 1971 after putting him on a treadmill to the barber shop. Copying Garry Unger has become virtually a symbolic battle between the mods and the squares in a game where the squares, whether they care to admit it or not, are losing out.

Unger became significant because his hair is long and blond and—if you check with the women at any hockey rink—beautiful. The hair is so long that if you happened to look at Unger from behind and from the neck up you might think it was Goldilocks and start looking for the three bears.

To career hockey men who grew up in the boondocks of Northern Saskatchewan where brush-cuts were *"de rigueur,"* the Samson-like image of Garry Unger symbolized the revolution in hockey and they would have none of that. Punch Imlach rebelled against long-haired Maple Leafs and it was Imlach who eventually departed. Emile Francis denounced the long sideburns of Rod Gilbert and now Gilbert's mane rivals the flowing locks of Garry Unger; and where it will stop nobody knows.

"In my opinion," said Unger, "the length of my hair is irrelevant to hockey."

Garry has underlined his point by playing as well for the St. Louis Blues as he did with Detroit or Toronto when he looked more like Buster Brown than Derek Sanderson. But Unger's argument is meaningful because his emergence as a long-haired type who thinks nothing of wearing a purple and white prison stripe outfit on a golf course portrays the change in the modern hockey player. It's not just Unger or Sanderson or Gilbert. No, folks, the mods have come on strong. It's Bob Nevin, and J. C. Tremblay, Pierre Bouchard, Brad Park, Bobby Baun, and, well, you name him, and the chances are good he's got a touch of mod in him and his manager is gritting his teeth in dismay.

The mod stickhandler isn't merely mod on the outside. It's more than that; more like a state of mind. Take Bobby Baun, the robust Toronto Maple Leaf defenseman. Superficially he looks like a backwoods truckdriver, but Baun is a sensitive type whose interests center on gourmet cooking and the study of fine wines. And not casually either. He spent three weeks taking a *"Cordon Bleu"* course in preparing superior French cuisine and then went about the business of designing the kitchen in his home on a 100-acre farm 30 miles east of Toronto.

"The kitchen," said Baun, "has the same kind of setup you'd find in a small but very good restaurant."

Esoteric, yes. Bizarre for a professional hockey player, no.

"Cooking," Baun explained, "is very much like hockey. You've got to have a bit of an edge going in. And you've got to be excited about what you're doing. You've got to have those taste buds going for you, salivating a bit."

Baun isn't the only stickhandler with a fondness for good food. Both J. C. Tremblay and Pierre Bouchard of the Montreal Canadiens recently opened "haute cuisine" restaurants in their home town and, needless to say, Derek "Himself" Sanderson is involved with an eaterie or two in Boston.

Garry Unger notwithstanding, it was Sanderson who led the revolution in hockey styles when his colleagues meekly submitted to every general manager's command. It was Sanderson who showed up at the Bruins training camp in 1968 with long hair and sideburns. Milt Schmidt, the Boston manager, was furious. He demanded that Derek cut his sideburns. Sanderson refused. "How I play hockey is what you should worry about," said Derek. In time Derek was wearing bell-bottoms and Nehru jackets and giving his coach Harry Sinden conniptions. "What are you doing to me?" Sinden asked one day.

"I'm going to change things," said Sanderson. And he did. What's more, he knows he did. "Unger and Dave Keon followed me. Then even the diehard conservatives started to change." One of them was Bobby Orr. Derek decided he should look like Tarzan rather than Ensign Pulver. One day he took Orr aside and said:

"Bobby, the brushcut, forget it! It makes you look like a kid of sixteen."

Have you seen Orr lately? The hair would even make Tarzan proud.

If Sanderson revolutionized clothes and coiffure among hockey players, Ken Dryden put the accent on cerebral matters. The Montreal Canadiens goaltender startled the hockey world by taking a job with Ralph Naders "Raiders" during the summer of 1971.

To anyone who suggested it was a publicity stunt the answer to that was in Dryden's compensation—next to nothing—and the amount of work he invested, which was endless. He also prepared a paper, "Citizen Action in Canada," which deals with the cancer of public apathy.

"The idea," Dryden recently revealed, "is to look into the reason people choose not to become involved with issues."

Curiously, Ken's coach, Scotty Bowman, endorses his intellectual pursuits as a boon to his goalkeeping. "Dryden is able to bounce back from a strenuous road trip and come up fresh because he gets away from his hockey work. When he leaves the rink, he becomes involved with people whose main interests are not in hockey."

A similarly heady type is former Toronto, Detroit, and St. Louis defenseman Carl Brewer, who claims he first began retiring from hockey when he was 18 and has been retiring ever since. "The owners sit in their offices and play chess with players' lives," Brewer once philosophized. "So, I play my own game of chess. . . . I play chess with the owners."

Such candid comments are a facet of the mod hockey player. He says what he thinks and lets his opponents lump it if they don't like it. Take Brad Park, the Rangers defenseman, as an example. He published a book, *Play the*

Man, in which he lambastes the Stanley Cup champion Boston Bruins, certain sportswriters, and a referee.

"Boston," wrote Park, "is like the schoolyard bully. Push the little guy around as long as the little guy won't fight back. But when the little guy fights back, the bully doesn't know what to do. That happens to the Bruins."

Park and his Ranger teammates have been exposed to the mod world of Manhattan but their manager, Francis, has made a point to keep the players as far from it as possible. Nearly every Ranger lives in the small suburban community of Long Beach, which, in its way, is more like a Canadian hamlet than part of the bustling metropolis.

Only Rod Gilbert among the Rangers lives alone in a Manhattan apartment. He is a bachelor who once roomed with Bob Nevin before Nevin was traded to Minnesota. Sources close to the Rangers insist that Nevin's trade was traceable to his groovy life style that didn't endear him to Francis.

How come Gilbert remained? Part of the answer is in production and the other in the fact that managers have come to realize that they simply can't chuck an athlete because of his mod style, particularly if he's a veteran such as Gilbert. But there is no question that they try to control the rookies such as Carr.

Carr put that in perspective once when he compared himself with Gilbert. "I live on Long Beach," said the long-haired rookie. "Rod's been here ten years. I don't think Francis would like it if I moved into the city."

The mod emphasis in hockey has even gone a step farther recently—into movies. A full-length film, *Face-Off*, based on a book of the same name, was produced in Canada with the cooperation and participation of several NHL players including Jim McKenny of the Toronto Maple Leafs, Sanderson, and ex-Leaf captain George Armstrong. Here's what Clyde Gilmour, film critic for the Toronto *Daily Star*, had to say about it:

"There is plenty of explicit sex and a lot of totally plausible obscenity and profanity in the book. There is none in the movie, which has been purposely made 'clean,' so that junior and juvenile hockey fans among the ticket-buyers won't be blocked by a restricted rating."

Good, bad, or indifferent, the film points up another aspect of the mod syndrome and that is that hockey more and more has become a big-time entertainment commodity. Entertainers are in the mod world and hockey players can't escape it.

"Why do you think hockey players refuse to wear helmets," the business advisor of an NHL star said. "It's simple: they know they're more glamorous without them and that they can make more money with commercials. They have an identity. When they wear helmets they all look alike."

Money has been a factor, too. For the first time in the game's history, hockey players are mining the shekels. Mind you, not with the ease of baseball, football, or basketball players; but the money is coming in and all you have to do is look at Vic Hadfield's handsome wardrobe to know that Rod Gilbert isn't the only clothes-conscious Ranger.

Just where the trend will stop is anybody's guess. As Garry Unger once remarked: "What if the latest fashion became brush-cuts again? Would somebody order you to grow it long?"

WHY THERE ARE NO BLACKS IN THE NHL

QUITE a fuss was made when the New York Raiders of the World Hockey Association signed a black, Alton White, to a 1972-73 contract.

White, who learned his hockey after moving to Winnipeg at age eight, has relentlessly progressed up the hockey ladder ever since he turned pro with Fort Wayne of the International League in 1965-66. He played in Providence in the American League last season but never made it to the NHL. It was enough to make a man like Alton believe he deserved greater things. Only one black man has ever reached the NHL.

"I feel I'm a good hockey player," said the 28-year-old White. "I have a lot of confidence in myself and I believe that, given the opportunity, I'll be able to make it in the WHA if not the NHL."

Willie O'Ree was the first black to break the color

barrier with the Boston Bruins in 1960-61 after a two-game trial in 1957-58.

Now 39 years old, O'Ree is considered too old for another crack at the majors, but there are those who believe that with a break or two he could have lasted longer than one season.

"I never got a chance in my first tryout in Boston," said O'Ree, who played six years with San Diego of the Western League. "The second time around I had nobody to blame but myself. I had plenty of chances but I was up-tight, rushed things, and didn't get the goals I might have if I wasn't so overanxious."

The NHL was a six-team league then. Now there are 16 NHL clubs and the World Hockey Association. White wanted the NHL but he's delighted to be in the WHA.

"Right now," says White, "I look at the NHL rosters and see names like Guy Lapointe, Marc Tardif, Rejean Houle, Don Marcotte, Reg Leach, and Ken Dryden. These are people I've played against pretty well. I'm a hustler. A good skater. I'm not really that big so I have to rely mainly on skating and hustling. Compared with past years, I'm a lot more capable hockey player. I feel I'm a lot better than some guys in the NHL today."

The color of his skin is not regarded as any more of a detour for Alton than it was when he skated in the lower Canadian leagues. His first games were played in Amherst, Nova Scotia, but his family moved to Winnipeg when Alton was only eight.

"We had to move because my Dad was getting lung disease from working in the local foundry," White recalled. "He got a job as a sleeping car porter for the Canadian National Railroad and I grew up playing against NHL guys like Ted Irvine and Peter Stemkowski."

Alton graduated from midget hockey to the Winnipeg Rangers in the Manitoba Junior Hockey League. Former Buffalo skater Gordie Pennell coached the Winnipeg Rangers and molded Alton into a capable pro.

In 1965-66 he played for Fort Wayne in the International League and then three seasons with Columbus before moving up to Providence.

Like O'Ree, White isn't naive enough to believe his color is ignored by those who play against or watch him on the ice. Willie, of course, was the Jackie Robinson of hockey but the abuse was much lighter for O'Ree.

"Over the years," said Willie after leaving the Bruins, "a fan here, a player there has slurred me but there hasn't been much of it. In the NHL they rode me, but just like they would any other player. Sure, I've heard things. I've been booed a lot but I like to think it's because I was one of the stars of a rival team, not because of my color."

By contrast, White insists he's had few problems because of his color.

"Once in a while," Alton said, "I hear some wisecracks from people in the stands. But at least they know I'm out there working. I was very well accepted in Providence and haven't had any problems whatsoever. I get along well with all the people; the fans treat me exceptionally well."

If White had been owned outright by a club such as Pittsburgh, Buffalo, Los Angeles, or Philadelphia the chances are that he'd have been in the NHL.

"It was tough for me to go up," he said," because I was owned by Providence. So, in order for me to go up I'd have had to be sold. I got a little bit down when I saw guys go up when I knew I was a better hockey player. And they went up because they were owned by a different organization. Then along came the WHA and my big chance." The reason there are so few in pro hockey is that there are relatively few Negroes in Canada, from where most hockey players come.

In the off-season White works for his brother Ken's construction business in Vancouver. "I also like to work with kids," he said. "Maybe if I didn't like it in hockey I'd have wound up with a job as a recreation leader just to be near the youngsters."

Although there is no apparent discrimination against blacks in hockey today, it was not ever thus. During the mid and late forties an entire Negro Line consisting of the Carnegie Brothers, Ossie and Herbie, and Manny McIntyre, starred for Sherbrooke in the Quebec Senior Hockey League.

Herbie, regarded as the best of the three, was believed to be the equal of most NHL stars, but couldn't crack the majors. In an interview not long ago Herbie hinted that his skin color had more than a little to do with it.

Certainly, if the line was in its playing prime today it would be an instant hit in the NHL.

Never a star, O'Ree was given an NHL chance without any compunctions.

"There has never been the discrimination in hockey like there was in baseball," said O'Ree after his NHL chance. "I didn't face any of the very real problems that Jackie Robinson had to face."

Now that the NHL is planning expansion to 24 teams by the end of the seventies and more American-born players are being groomed for major league hockey, the inevitable question is whether a black skater from the United States will ever reach the NHL.

If the question had been asked five to ten years ago the answer would be an emphatic "No!" But recently more and more black youngsters have taken up hockey and with very positive results.

The municipally operated ice skating rink in Harlem currently has a full-scale hockey program and, judging by current production, should be sending a few boys to Canadian Junior Leagues within a few years. After that it's only a matter of time before they reach the top.

Jerry Rodelli, director of publicity for the Greater New York Ice Hockey League, reports that there are now more than 50 black skaters in that first-rate circuit.

"Ronnie Fortt, a 16-year-old center," said Rodelli, "shows exceptional skill as a skater. With continued hard work it's entirely possible that he could go all the way. His coach, Eddie Eskanzi, believes that Fortt is an exceptional young prospect."

And if Ronnie needs any inspiration all he has to do is watch Alton White at Madison Square Garden.

THOSE FUNNY FANS

THERE are times when the people who pay to watch hockey games put on a better show than the players themselves. Observers differ as to which city has the wildest spectators in the NHL but those from Boston, Chicago, and St. Louis rank at the top of the list.

For many years Bruin followers suffered through some of the worst hockey ever seen in any NHL city. Nevertheless, they still kept coming and, somehow, managed to retain their sense of humor. During the early sixties, when the Bruins were at their lowest ebb, the Boston sextet received "help" from an unexpected source.

On a Monday morning following the usual Sunday night Boston defeat, a fan named Sandy turned up at the then coach Milt Schmidt's office. "I want a tryout with the Bruins," he insisted. "I've seen your team play and I think I can make the club."

Schmidt wasn't about to dismiss a philanthropist without a hearing. "How old are you? Who have you played for? What makes you think you can play in the NHL?"

Sandy listened intently and then replied, "I san skate faster than anyone on the Bruins and I'll bet $10 I can."

Intrigued by the man's gall, Schmidt suggested that Sandy return home and pick up his skates. Yes, he was willing to accept the challenge.

Sandy showed up the following morning with a pair of skates that had not been sharpened in two years. Bruins trainer Dan Canney took care of that and then Sandy was ready to take the ice. "What's your position?" asked Schmidt.

"Wing," said Sandy. So Schmidt decided to go along with the gag.

Murray Oliver, then the Bruins center, started a rush toward goalie Ed Johnston. Johnny Bucyk was on the left and Sandy on the right. When they arrived to within ten feet of the goalie Oliver slipped a perfect pass to Sandy. Precisely at that moment, Johnston stepped aside, leaving nothing but an open net for the skating fan. Sandy took a swipe at it but missed the puck and crashed into the end boards.

"I guess I'm really a defenseman," Sandy advised Schmidt.

The coach obliged and decided to pair him with the veteran Leo Boivin.

Their first challenge was a three-man rush by the Oliver line. As Bucyk and Oliver picked up speed, Boivin began shouting at Sandy. "Back up, boy, back up!"

"For what?" demanded Sandy. But before he could finish his question the Oliver line had skated past them and scored a goal.

Schmidt wasn't about to give up on his prospect. "Now's your chance," said Schmidt, "pick a player and he'll race you for the ten-dollar bet."

"Never mind a player," said Sandy, "I'll race you instead."

"Okay," said Schmidt, "let's go."

Suddenly, the exuberant rooter reconsidered. "Ah, never mind," he insisted. "I don't want to embarrass anyone."

By contrast, Chicago fans would think nothing of embarrassing their own. "There was a fellow in the balcony," recalled ex-Black Hawk publicist Johnny Gottselig, "with a fedora on the end of a fishing line. He'd fire it onto the ice and then he'd haul it back up. One night he blew the whole thing. As he reeled in the hat, Frank Mahovlich, when he was with the Maple Leafs, swiped at it with his stick and snapped it off the line."

At the time Gottselig also was handling the radio play-by-play for the Black Hawks.

"In those days," said Gottselig, "the broadcasts were sponsored by White Owl cigars. One night I was doing the game when right in front of me, dangling from a line, were half-a-dozen Phillie's cigars. Well, I knew that most of those people brought transistor radios to the game so they can listen as well as watch, so I made a point of saying 'make sure you get your White Owls on the way home.'

"The next game the line came down from above with a whole box of White Owls."

Gottselig remembered when a fan showed up at Chicago Stadium with a six-foot-six dummy of Mahovlich with a hangman's rope around his neck. "He wanted to hang Big M in effigy from the top balcony," said Gottselig. "We had to take it away from him. From that height it could have been dangerous if it fell on anybody."

It is generally conceded that hockey fans in Montreal and Toronto are the most decorous in the NHL. "They go to a game as if they're going to the opera," said Weston Adams, Jr., president of the Bruins. "Our fans can be a little rougher."

Others consider that an understatement. Pat Jordan, an

author who had never been to Boston until the 1969-70 season, was astonished at the behavior of Bruins fans. "They do not come to their Garden for comfort," said Jordan. "Nor do they come after a fine dinner and cocktails like New York Rangers fans go to their Garden. Boston fans come after an argument with their wives, their dinners pushed aside in anger. They come not to complement a good day, but in one last angry attempt to 'get even' with another in a long line of very bad days."

During the early fifties the "Gallery Gods" in New York hurled so much abuse at defenseman Allan Stanley that manager Frank Boucher felt obliged to trade him to Chicago; he played excellent hockey there and later continued to do so at Toronto.

Montreal fans have been equally harsh on some of their own players. "They generally are more patient with a French-Canadian player," said former Canadiens' managing director Frank Selke, Sr. "But they show much less tolerance towards Anglo-Saxons."

As a result, Selke once was forced to do to his left wing Ab McDonald what Boucher did to Stanley. McDonald was dealt to the Black Hawks where he, too, became a star. "If Ab had stayed here," said Selke, "the fans would have ruined his morale. He would have been no good to anybody, including himself."

When McDonald returned to the Montreal Forum in a Chicago uniform a few weeks later he scored the winning goal for the Black Hawks and the Montreal fans hailed him with a hefty round of applause. "First they chase him out of Montreal," Selke lamented, "and now they applaud him!"

THINGS YOU NEVER KNEW ABOUT EQUIPMENT

THE shot came high from the stick of forward Larry Mickey and it had a murderous look about it.

But like a guided missile on high, it appeared innocent enough from a distance. The hockey puck, six ounces of hard vulcanized rubber, blurred through the air. It was meant to go into the net behind Gilles Villemure, the New York Rangers goaltender, who is paid something like $40,000 to stop these devastating little missiles with his body.

For a split-second Villemure lost sight of the hard piece of rubber. It was too late. Like a chunk of flak the puck slammed at about 95 m.p.h. into his neck and all 5-8 and 170 pounds of Villemure crashed limply to the ice. "At first," said a teammate, "I thought he was dead."

Villemure survived, but the episode dramatized the vulnerability of hockey players—especially goaltenders—to injury in what is the world's fastest major sport. It is a vulnerability so great that on a goaltender, for example, a piece of protective equipment has been designed for every portion of the body—except the neck.

"What we really need," says goalie Gerry Cheevers of the Stanley Cup champion Boston Bruins, "is something like an armored diver's helmet which would cover *every-thing* from the top of our head down to our neck."

Eventually this may happen, because the design of new hockey equipment follows demand. It also may explain why hockey players are the most armored men in sports.

It wasn't always this way.

In fact up until the mid-twenties, goaltenders were frighteningly ill-protected from the missiles headed their way. For leg protection they wore nothing but borrowed cricket pads and might still be wearing them today were it not for Pop Kenesky, an inventive Hamilton, Ontario, harness-maker who designed a pad which was wider and stuck out at the sides instead of going around the leg.

Pretty soon the National Hockey League goaltenders heard about Pop Kenesky's invention and they began buying them. Today 95-year-old tobacco-spitting Pop Kenesky hand-makes the pads for every goaltender in professional hockey and for several players in Europe. His design has been somewhat modified by the Gerry Cosby Sporting Goods firm in New York City.

Amazingly, the contemporary goalie pad differs little from the original model. Its width has been trimmed from 12 to 10 inches by league rule and some minor modifications have been made to suit particular goalies. But Pop, who makes 300 pairs a year—and charges approximately

$140 a set—warns against tampering with his basic design.

Once Harvey Teno, a capable American League goalie, warned Pop that he was putting too much padding in the pads. Kenesky said he wasn't, but to please Teno he made a lighter pad.

"Next thing I knew," said Pop, "he got hit in one of the weak spots and the poor guy quit hockey."

The Kenesky pad worn by goalies Villemure and Ed Giacomin of the Rangers contains three pieces of cream-colored horsehide, felt, rubberized canvas, and special stuffing. The sides are stuffed with deer hair and the front with kapok. According to Kenesky, the deer hair is light and provides top protection when stuffed hard. "On account of the slapshot, which comes so so fast," said Pop, "I stuff the pads harder than I did years ago."

Pop doesn't care to fool with unorthodox requests if he can help it but he had some dandies in his day.

When Earl Robertson tended goal for the old New York Americans he made a rare request of Kenesky and Pop obliged. Robertson wanted a rabbit's foot stuffed into each pad. Another time, Pop put together a set of pads made out of goatskin for Johnny Bower of the Toronto Maple Leafs, but the process turned out to be too costly.

A more practical suggestion was made by Harry Lumley, then with the Detroit Red Wings. He disliked the straight up-and-down quality of the pads and asked Pop to build in a pocket at the shins—goalies call it a "scoop"— so that the puck drops straight to the ice when hitting it instead of rebounding to an opponent. Lumley's idea has been built into almost every pad since then.

Some goaltenders have become so enamored with their Kenesky pads they refuse to obtain new ones, although the team would foot the bill. Bill Durnan of the Montreal Canadiens won six Vezina Trophies before he even *thought* about a new set of pads. Each spring he'd send his old set to the Kenesky shop in Hamilton, Ontario, and have them repaired. One year Pop's son, Frank, who also works for the business, suggested that Durnan try a new pair. "Y'know," the goalie shot back, "it's a good idea— but I'm quitting after this season. It would take me a whole year to break in a new set of pads."

Next to the goal pads the most personalized piece of

hockey equipment is the goalie's face-mask, which now is worn by all but one—Gump Worsley of Minnesota—regular netminders in the NHL. A Massachusetts manufacturer as well as several NHL trainers have become known for their mask design, but nobody has cornered the market like Pop Kenesky.

The goalie mask still remains a contentious piece of equipment, on the grounds that it cuts off an all-important angle at the skate level. "I never got around to trying a mask," said the 43-year-old Worsley, "and I'll stay without it until I quit."

Jacques Plante, currently the Toronto Maple Leafs goalie, is the man who introduced the mask to regular goaltending use while he was playing for New York. A shot by Andy Bathgate nearly decapitated Plante at Madison Square Garden and he left the ice smeared with blood.

"I never saw the shot that smashed into my face," said Plante. "When they stitched me up, Toe Blake, the Canadiens coach, asked me if I would go back in. I said only if I could wear the mask which I had worn in our workouts. He okayed it and I played. I must have been a sight. The mask was crude, I was patched up, and there was just enough blood on my face to complete the picture.

"Later in the season I was in a slump and Blake asked if I'd mind taking off the mask, to regain my touch. I took it off one night in Detroit and they got three goals. After the game, Blake came over to me and said: 'Put the mask back on. I don't want to shoulder the blame if you get injured without it.' We began to roll after that game and went on to win the Stanley Cup in eight straight games. Since then the mask has been refined. It's stronger and lighter. A few years ago in the playoffs a shot by Fred Stanfield of Boston hit me right smack in the mask. If it wasn't for that protection I'd be dead today."

In addition to the mask and pads, goaltenders also are unique among hockey players in that they wear a thick, baseball-catcher-like chest protector under their jerseys. Their gloves also differ, one being similar to a first-baseman's mitt—the better to nab the shots—and the other a rectangular piece of leather designed to deflect pucks out of danger.

Because he uses his skates to block shots primarily, and

does little actual free-skating in comparison with his team-mates, the goalie uses a decidely different skate than his forwards or defensemen.

The traditional hockey skate blade is supported by two tubes at each end, connecting with the tubular blade. The goalie's skates are tubeless, consisting of one long blade—reminiscent of an old-fashioned skate—stretching from in front of the boot to the back. The upper side of the blade has several tongues of steel extending upward from the bottom to prevent pucks from slipping through the opening between the blade and the bottom· of the skate boot. Since the pucks often strike the goalie's boot at speeds of upwards of 120 m.p.h., a thick fibre covering protects each boot from the steel reinforced boxed toe back to the heel.

Curiously, few goalies in the NHL wear a helmet to protect the top of their heads but more and more forwards and defensemen are wearing the device. Since the death of Minnesota's Bill Masterton following a collision on the ice at Metropolitan Sports Center, a clamor has persisted to make helmets mandatory in the NHL. Yet owners and managers—who believe players appear more glamorous and appealing without a helmet—insist that the choice should be a personal one made by the players themselves.

As a result, most NHL players refuse to wear the helmets, which is curious since helmets have been a vital part of football equipment since Pudge Hefflefinger, the last of the bareheaded breed, retired in 1898.

The complaint about hockey helmets is that they (a) are too cumbersome, (b) are too hot, (c) are too loose, and (d) curb one's hearing potential. In addition there is a certain psychological masculine element involved.

Larry Zeidel, who played pro hockey for more than 20 years, accumulated two fractured skulls and more than 200 stitches in his head alone, yet he never accepted a helmet as a regular piece of equipment.

"Nobody else wore one," said Zeidel, now a Philadelphia stockbroker, "so, naturally, I didn't want to be the first!"

THE STATISTICS

APPS, SYLVANUS MARSHALL (SYL) JR.

Born, Toronto, Ont., August 1, 1947.
Center. Shoots right. 6', 185 lbs.
Last amateur club: Kingston Frontenacs (Srs.).

Season	Club	Lea	Regular Schedule					Playoffs				
			GP	G	A	TP	PIM	GP	G	A	TP	PIM
1968-69	Buffalo	AHL	2	1	2	3	4	--	--	--	--	--
1969-70	Omaha	CHL	68	16	38	54	43	12	*10	9	*19	4
1969-70	Buffalo	AHL	--	--	--	--	--	7	2	3	5	6
1970-71	NY Rangers	NHL	31	1	2	3	11	--	--	--	--	--
1970-71	Omaha	CHL	11	0	5	5	4	--	--	--	--	--
1970-71	Pittsburgh	NHL	31	9	16	25	21	--	--	--	--	--
1971-72	Pittsburgh	NHL	72	15	44	59	78	4	1	0	1	2
	NHL Totals		134	25	62	87	110	4	1	0	1	2

Traded to **Pittsburgh** by **New York** for Glen Sather, January 26, 1971.

BERENSON, GORDON ARTHUR (RED)

Born, Regina, Sask., December 8, 1939.
Center. Shoots left. 6', 190 lbs.
Last amateur club: University of Michigan.

Season	Club	Lea	Regular Schedule					Playoffs				
			GP	G	A	TP	PIM	GP	G	A	TP	PIM
1961-62	Mtl. Canadiens	NHL	4	1	2	3	4	5	2	0	2	0
1962-63	Hull-Ottawa	EPHL	30	23	25	48	28	--	--	--	--	--
1962-63	Mtl. Canadiens	NHL	37	2	6	8	15	5	0	0	0	0
1963-64	Mtl. Canadiens	NHL	69	7	9	16	12	7	0	0	0	4
1964-65	Quebec	AHL	65	22	34	56	16	5	1	2	3	8
1964-65	Mtl. Canadiens	NHL	3	1	2	3	0	9	0	1	1	2
1965-66	Quebec	AHL	34	17	36	53	14	6	1	5	6	2
1965-66	Mtl. Canadiens	NHL	23	3	4	7	12	--	--	--	--	--
1966-67	NY Rangers	NHL	30	0	5	5	2	4	0	1	1	2
1967-68	NY Rangers	NHL	19	2	1	3	2	--	--	--	--	--
	St. Louis	NHL	55	22	29	51	22	18	5	2	7	9
1968-69	St. Louis	NHL	76	35	47	82	43	12	7	3	10	20
1969-70	St. Louis	NHL	67	33	39	72	38	16	7	5	12	8
1970-71	St. Louis	NHL	45	16	26	42	12	--	--	--	--	--
	Detroit	NHL	24	5	12	17	4	--	--	--	--	--
1971-72	Detroit	NHL	78	28	41	69	16	--	--	--	--	--
	NHL Totals		530	155	223	378	182	76	21	12	33	45

Traded by **Montreal** to **New York** for Ted Taylor and Garry Peters, June 13, 1966. Traded by **New York** with Barclay Plager to **St. Louis** for Ron Stewart and Ron Attwell, November 29, 1967. Traded to **Detroit** by **St. Louis** with Tim Ecclestone for Garry Unger and Wayne Connelly, February 6, 1971.

CLARKE, ROBERT EARLE (BOBBY)

Born, Flin Flon, Man., August 13, 1949.
Center. Shoots right. 5'10", 180 lbs.
Last amateur club: Flin Flon Bombers (Jrs.).

Season	Club	Lea	Regular Schedule					Playoffs				
			GP	G	A	TP	PIM	GP	G	A	TP	PIM
1969-70	Philadelphia	NHL	76	15	31	46	68	—	—	—	—	—
1970-71	Philadelphia	NHL	77	27	36	63	78	4	0	0	0	0
1971-72	Philadelphia	NHL	78	35	46	81	87	—	—	—	—	—
		HHL Totals	231	77	113	190	233	4	0	0	0	0

COURNOYER, YVAN SERGE

Born, Drummondville, Que., November 22, 1943.
Right wing. Shoots left. 5'7", 165 lbs.
Last amateur club: Canadians (Jrs.).

Season	Club	Lea	Regular Schedule					Playoffs				
			GP	G	A	TP	PIM	GP	G	A	TP	PIM
1963-64	Mtl. Canadiens	NHL	5	4	0	4	0	—	—	—	—	—
1964-65	Quebec	AHL	7	2	1	3	0	—	—	—	—	—
1964-65	Mtl. Canadiens	NHL	55	7	10	17	10	12	3	1	4	0
1965-66	Mtl. Canadiens	NHL	65	18	11	29	8	10	2	3	5	2
1966-67	Mtl. Canadiens	NHL	69	25	15	40	14	10	2	3	5	6
1967-68	Mtl. Canadiens	NHL	64	28	32	60	23	13	6	8	14	4
1968-69	Mtl. Canadiens	NHL	76	43	44	87	31	14	4	7	11	5
1969-70	Mtl. Canadiens	NHL	72	27	36	63	23	—	—	—	—	—
1970-71	Mtl. Canadiens	NHL	65	37	36	73	21	20	10	12	22	6
1971-72	Mtl. Canadiens	NHL	73	47	36	83	15	6	2	1	3	2
		NHL Totals	544	236	220	456	145	85	29	35	64	25

DRYDEN, KENNETH WAYNE (KEN)

Born, Hamilton, Ont., August 8, 1947.
Goaltender. Shoots left. 6'4", 210 lbs.
Last amateur club: Canadian National Team.

Season	Club	Lea	Regular Schedule					Playoffs				
			GPI	MINS	GA	SO	GAPG	GPI	MINS	GA	SO	GAPG
1970-71	Mtl. Voyageurs	AHL	33	1899	84	3	2.68	—	—	—	—	—
1970-71ab	Mtl. Canadiens	NHL	6	327	9	0	1.65	20	1221	61	0	3.00
1971-72c	Mtl. Canadiens	NHL	64	3800	142	8	2.24	6	360	18	0	
		NHL Totals	70	4127	151	8	2.16	26	1581	79	0	3.00

a Received one assist in playoffs.
b Won Conn Smythe Trophy.

ESPOSITO, PHILIP ANTHONY (PHIL)

Born, Sault Ste Marie, Ont., February 20, 1942.
Center. Shoots left. 6'1", 120 lbs.
Last amateur club: St. Catherines (Jrs.).

Season	Club	Lea	Regular Schedule					Playoffs				
			GP	G	A	TP	PIM	GP	G	A	TP	PIM
1961-62	Sault Ste. Marie	EPHL	6	0	3	3	2	—	—	—	—	—
1962-63	St. Louis	EPHL	71	36	54	90	51	—	—	—	—	—
1963-64	St. Louis	CPHL	43	26	54	80	65	—	—	—	—	—
1963-64	Chicago	NHL	27	3	2	5	2	4	0	0	0	0
1964-65	Chicago	NHL	70	23	32	55	44	13	3	3	6	15
1965-66	Chicago	NHL	69	27	26	53	49	6	1	1	2	2
1966-67	Chicago	NHL	69	21	40	61	40	6	0	0	0	7
1967-68	Boston	NHL	74	35	*49	84	21	4	0	3	3	0
1968-69ab	Boston	NHL	74	49	*77	*126	79	10	*8	*10	*18	8
1969-70d	Boston	NHL	76	*43	56	99	50	14	*13	*14	*27	16
1970-71ace	Boston	NHL	78	*76	76	*152	71	7	3	7	10	6
1971-72a	Boston	NHL	76	66	67	133	76	15	9	15	24	24
		NHL Totals	613	343	425	768	432	79	37	53	90	78

a Won Art Ross Trophy.
b Won Hart Trophy.
c NHL record for points in regular season.
d NHL record for points in Stanley Cup Playoffs (shared with Frank Mahovlich).
e NHL record for goals in regular season.
Traded to Boston by Chicago with Ken Hodge and Fred Stanfield for Gilles
Marotte, Pit Martin and Jack Norris, May 15, 1967.

GIACOMIN, EDWARD

Born, Sudbury, Ont., June 6, 1939.
Goaltender. Shoots left. 5'11", 175 lbs.
Last amateur club: New York Rovers (EHL).

Season	Club	Lea	Regular Schedule					Playoffs				
			GPI	MINS	GA	SO	GAPG	GPI	MINS	GA	SO	GAPG
1959-60	Providence	AHL	1	—	4	0	4.00	—	—	—	—	—
1960-61	Providence	AHL	43	—	183	0	4.26	—	—	—	—	—
1961-62	Providence	AHL	40	—	144	2	3.60	—	—	—	—	—
1962-63	Providence	AHL	39	—	102	4	2.62	6	—	31	0	5.17
1963-64a	Providence	AHL	69	—	232	*6	3.37	3	—	12	0	4.00
1964-65	Providence	AHL	59	—	226	0	3.84	—	—	—	—	—
1965-66	NY Rangers	NHL	36	2096	128	0	3.66	—	—	—	—	—
1965-66	Baltimore	AHL	7	—	21	0	3.00	—	—	—	—	—
1966-67	NY Rangers	NHL	68	3981	173	*9	2.61	4	246	14	0	3.41
1967-68	NY Rangers	NHL	66	3940	160	*8	2.44	6	360	18	0	3.00
1968-69	NY Rangers	NHL	70	4114	175	7	2.55	3	180	10	0	3.33
1969-70a	NY Rangers	NHL	70	4148	163	6	2.36	5	276	19	0	4.13
1970-71b	NY Rangers	NHL	45	2641	95	*8	2.15	12	759	28	0	2.21
1971-72	NY Rangers	NHL	44	2551	115	1	2.70	10	600	27	0	2.70
		NHL Totals	399	21471	1009	39	2.53	40	2421	149	0	3.73

a Received two assists.
b Shared Vezina Trophy with Gilles Villemure.

HENDERSON, PAUL GARNET

Born, Kincardine, Ont., January 28, 1943.
Left wing. Shoots right. 5'11", 180 lbs.
Last amateur club: Hamilton Red Wings (Jrs.).

Season	Club	Lea	Regular Schedule					Playoffs				
			GP	G	A	TP	PIM	GP	G	A	TP	PIM
1962-63	Detroit	NHL	2	0	0	0	9	—	—	—	—	—
1963-64	Pittsburgh	AHL	38	10	14	24	18	—	—	—	—	—
1963-64	Detroit	NHL	32	3	3	6	14	14	2	3	5	6
1964-65	Detroit	NHL	70	8	13	21	30	7	0	2	2	0
1965-66	Detroit	NHL	69	22	24	46	34	12	3	3	6	10
1966-67	Detroit	NHL	46	21	19	40	10	—	—	—	—	—
1967-68	Detroit	NHL	50	13	20	33	35	—	—	—	—	—
	Toronto	NHL	13	5	6	11	8	—	—	—	—	—
1968-69	Toronto	NHL	74	27	32	59	16	4	0	1	1	0
1969-70	Toronto	NHL	67	20	22	42	18	—	—	—	—	—
1970-71	Toronto	NHL	72	30	30	60	34	6	5	1	6	4
1971-72	Toronto	NHL	73	38	19	57	32	5	1	2	3	6
	NHL Totals		568	187	188	375	240	48	11	12	23	26

Traded to Toronto by Detroit with Norm Ullman and Floyd Smith for Frank Mahovlich, Pete Stemkowski, Garry Unger and the rights to Carl Brewer, March 3, 1968.

HULL, ROBERT MARVIN (BOBBY)

Born, Point Anne, Ont., January 3, 1939.
Left wing. Shoots left. 5'10", 193 lbs.
Last amateur club: St. Catherines (Jrs.).

Season	Club	Lea	Regular Schedule					Playoffs				
			GP	G	A	TP	PIM	GP	G	A	TP	PIM
1957-58	Chicago	NHL	70	13	34	47	62	—	—	—	—	—
1958-59	Chicago	NHL	70	18	32	50	50	6	1	1	2	2
1959-60a	Chicago	NHL	70	*39	42	*81	68	3	1	0	1	2
1960-61	Chicago	NHL	67	31	25	56	43	12	4	10	14	4
1961-62a	Chicago	NHL	70	*50	34	*84	35	12	*8	5	13	4
1962-63	Chicago	NHL	65	31	31	62	27	5	*8	2	10	4
1963-64	Chicago	NHL	70	*43	44	87	50	7	2	5	7	2
1964-65bc	Chicago	NHL	61	39	32	71	32	14	*10	7	*17	27
1965-66ac	Chicago	NHL	65	*54	43	*97	70	6	2	2	4	10
1966-67	Chicago	NHL	66	*52	28	80	52	6	4	2	6	0
1967-68	Chicago	NHL	71	*44	31	75	39	11	4	6	10	15
1968-69	Chicago	NHL	74	*58	49	107	48	—	—	—	—	—
1969-70	Chicago	NHL	61	38	29	67	8	8	3	8	11	2
1970-71	Chicago	NHL	78	44	52	96	32	18	11	14	25	16
1971-72	Chicago	NHL	78	50	43	93	24	8	4	4	8	6
	NHL Totals		1036	604	549	1153	640	116	62	66	128	100

a Won Art Ross Trophy.
b Won Lady Byng Memorial Trophy.
c Won Hart Trophy.
Transferred to Winnipeg Jets of World Hockey Ass'n, summer of 1972.

KURTENBACH, ORLAND JOHN

Born, Cudworth, Sask., September 7, 1936.
Center. Shoots left. 6'2", 195 lbs.
Last amateur club: Prince Albert Mintos (Jr.).

			Regular Schedule					Playoffs				
Season	Club	Lea	GP	G	A	TP	PIM	GP	G	A	TP	PIM
1954-55	Saskatoon	WHL	1	0	0	0	0	—	—	—	—	—
1955-56	Saskatoon	WHL	3	0	0	0	4	2	0	0	0	0
1957-58a	Vancouver	WHL	52	15	39	54	58	8	3	3	6	8
1958-59	Buffalo	AHL	70	9	14	23	73	7	0	0	0	0
1959-60	Springfield	AHL	14	0	6	6	17	—	—	—	—	—
1959-60	Vancouver	WHL	42	11	27	38	51	11	1	5	6	11
1960-61	NY Rangers	NHL	10	0	6	6	2	—	—	—	—	—
1960-61	Vancouver	WHL	55	20	27	47	31	—	—	—	—	—
1961-62	Boston	NHL	8	0	0	0	6	—	—	—	—	—
1961-62	Providence	AHL	64	31	33	64	51	3	1	1	2	5
1962-63	San Francisco	WHL	70	30	57	87	94	17	4	13	17	*51
1963-64	Boston	NHL	70	12	25	37	91	—	—	—	—	—
1964-65	Boston	NHL	64	6	20	26	86	—	—	—	—	—
1965-66	Toronto	NHL	70	9	6	15	54	4	0	0	0	20
1966-67	NY Rangers	NHL	60	11	25	36	58	3	0	2	2	0
1967-68	NY Rangers	NHL	73	15	20	35	82	6	1	0	1	26
1968-69	NY Rangers	NHL	2	0	0	0	2	—	—	—	—	—
1968-69	Omaha	CHL	1	0	0	0	0	—	—	—	—	—
1969-70	Buffalo	AHL	6	1	5	6	2	—	—	—	—	—
1969-70	NY Rangers	NHL	53	4	10	14	47	6	1	2	3	24
1970-71	Vancouver	NHL	52	21	32	53	84	—	—	—	—	—
1971-72	Vancouver	NHL	78	24	37	61	48	—	—	—	—	—
		NHL Totals	540	102	181	283	560	19	2	4	6	70

a Won WHL (Coast Division) Rookie Award.
Drafted by Boston from Rangers, June 1961. Traded by Boston with Pat Stapleton and Andy Hebenton to Toronto for Ron Stewart, June 8, 1965. Drafted by New York from Toronto, June 15, 1966. Drafted by Vancouver from New York in Expansion Draft, June 10, 1970.

LAPOINTE, GUY GERARD

Born, Montreal, Que., March 18, 1948.
Defense. Shoots left. 6', 185 lbs.
Last amateur club: Montreal Canadiens (Jrs.).

			Regular Schedule					Playoffs				
Season	Club	Lea	GP	G	A	TP	PIM	GP	G	A	TP	PIM
1968-69	Mtl. Canadiens	NHL	1	0	0	0	2	—	—	—	—	—
1968-69	Houston	CHL	65	3	15	18	120	3	1	0	1	6
1969-70	Mtl. Canadiens	NHL	5	0	0	0	4	—	—	—	—	—
1969-70	Mtl. Voyageurs	AHL	57	8	30	38	92	8	3	5	8	6
1970-71	Mtl. Canadiens	NHL	78	15	29	44	107	20	4	5	9	34
1971-72	Mtl. Canadiens	NHL	69	11	38	49	58	6	0	1	1	0
		NHL Totals	153	26	67	93	171	26	4	6	10	34

MAHOVLICH, PETER JOSEPH (PETE)

Born, Timmins, Ont., October 10, 1946.
Left wing. Shoots left. 6'5", 205 lbs.
Last amateur club: Hamilton (Jrs.).

Season	Club	Lea	Regular Schedule					Playoffs				
			GP	G	A	TP	PIM	GP	G	A	TP	PIM
1965-66	Detroit	NHL	3	0	1	1	0	—	—	—	—	—
1966-67	Detroit	NHL	34	1	3	4	16	—	—	—	—	—
1966-67	Pittsburgh	AHL	18	4	7	11	37	9	0	0	0	2
1967-68	Detroit	NHL	15	6	4	10	13	—	—	—	—	—
1967-68	Fort Worth	CPHL	42	20	14	34	103	—	—	—	—	—
1968-69	Fort Worth	CHL	34	19	17	36	54	—	—	—	—	—
1968-69	Detroit	NHL	30	2	2	4	21	—	—	—	—	—
1969-70	Mtl. Voyageurs	AHL	31	21	19	40	77	—	—	—	—	—
1969-70	Mtl. Canadiens	NHL	36	9	8	17	51	—	—	—	—	—
1970-71	Mtl. Canadiens	NHL	78	35	26	61	181	20	10	6	16	43
1971-72	Mtl. Canadiens	NHL	75	35	32	67	103	6	0	2	2	12
	NHL Totals		271	88	76	164	385	26	10	8	18	55

Traded to Montreal by Detroit with Bart Crashley for Garry Monahan and Doug Piper, June 6, 1969.

MAHOVLICH, FRANCIS WILLIAM (FRANK)

Born, Timmins, Ont., January 10, 1938.
Left wing. Shoots left. 6', 205 lbs.
Last amateur club: St. Michael's College (Jrs.).

Season	Club	Lea	Regular Schedule					Playoffs				
			GP	G	A	TP	PIM	GP	G	A	TP	PIM
1956-57	Toronto	NHL	3	1	0	1	2	—	—	—	—	—
1957-58a	Toronto	NHL	67	20	16	36	67	—	—	—	—	—
1958-59	Toronto	NHL	63	22	27	49	94	12	6	5	11	18
1959-60	Toronto	NHL	70	18	21	39	61	10	3	1	4	27
1960-61	Toronto	NHL	70	48	36	84	131	5	1	1	2	6
1961-62	Toronto	NHL	70	33	38	71	87	12	6	6	12	*29
1962-63	Toronto	NHL	67	36	37	73	56	9	0	2	2	8
1963-64	Toronto	NHL	70	26	29	55	66	14	4	*11	15	20
1964-65	Toronto	NHL	59	23	28	51	76	6	0	3	3	9
1965-66	Toronto	NHL	68	32	24	56	68	4	1	0	1	10
1966-67	Toronto	NHL	63	18	28	46	44	12	3	7	10	8
1967-68	Toronto	NHL	50	19	17	36	30	—	—	—	—	—
	Detroit	NHL	13	7	9	16	2	—	—	—	—	—
1968-69	Detroit	NHL	76	49	29	78	38	—	—	—	—	—
1969-70	Detroit	NHL	74	38	32	70	59	4	0	0	0	2
1970-71bc	Detroit	NHL	35	14	18	32	30	—	—	—	—	—
	Mtl. Canadiens	NHL	38	17	24	41	11	20	*14	13	*27	18
1971-72	Mtl. Canadiens	NHL	76	43	53	96	36	6	3	2	5	2
	NHL Totals		1032	454	466	930	958	114	41	51	92	157

a Won Calder Memorial Trophy.
b NHL record for goals in Stanley Cup Playoffs.
c NHL record for points in Stanley Cup Playoffs (shared with Phil Esposito).
Traded to Detroit by Toronto with Garry Unger, Pete Stemkowski and rights to Carl Brewer for Paul Henderson, Norm Ullman and Floyd Smith, March 3, 1968. Traded to Montreal by Detroit for Mickey Redmond, Guy Charron and Bill Collins, January 13, 1971.

McKENZIE, JOHN ALBERT
Born, High River, Alta., December 12, 1937.
Right wing. Shoots right. 5'9", 175 lbs.
Last amateur club: St. Catharines (Jrs.).

Season	Club	Lea	Regular Schedule					Playoffs				
			GP	G	A	TP	PIM	GP	G	A	TP	PIM
1955-56	Calgary	WHL	1	0	0	0	0	2	0	1	*1	2
1958-59	Calgary	WHL	13	2	5	7	18	—	—	—	—	—
1958-59	Chicago	NHL	32	3	4	7	22	2	0	0	0	2
1959-60	Detroit	NHL	59	8	12	20	50	2	0	0	0	0
1960-61	Detroit	NHL	16	3	1	4	13	—	—	—	—	—
1960-61	Hershey	AHL	47	19	23	42	84	8	3	6	9	10
1961-62	Hershey	AHL	58	30	29	59	149	7	1	2	3	19
1962-63a	Buffalo	AHL	71	35	46	81	122	13	8	12	*20	28
1963-64	Chicago	NHL	45	9	9	18	50	4	0	1	1	6
1964-65	St. Louis	CPHL	5	5	4	9	17	—	—	—	—	—
1964-65	Chicago	NHL	51	8	10	18	46	11	0	1	1	6
1965-66	NY Rangers	NHL	35	6	5	11	36	—	—	—	—	—
	Boston	NHL	36	13	9	22	36	—	—	—	—	164
1966-67	Boston	NHL	69	17	19	36	98	—	—	—	—	164
1967-68	Boston	NHL	74	28	38	66	107	4	1	1	2	8
1968-69	Boston	NHL	60	29	27	56	99	10	2	2	4	17
1969-70	Boston	NHL	72	29	41	70	114	14	5	12	17	35
1970-71	Boston	NHL	65	31	46	77	120	7	2	3	5	22
1971-72	Boston	NHL	77	22	47	69	126	15	5	12	17	37
	NHL Totals		691	206	268	474	917	69	15	32	47	133

a AHL Calder Cup Playoff Scoring Record held jointly with Zellio Toppazzini.
Drafted by Detroit from Chicago, June 1959. Traded by Detroit with Len Lunde Chicago for Doug Barkley, June 6, 1962. Traded by Chicago with Ray Cullen to New York for Tracy Pratt, Dick Meissner, Dave Richardson and Mel Pearson, June 4, 1965. Traded by New York to Boston for Reg Fleming, January 10, 1966. Transferred to player-coach of Philadelphia Blazers of World Hockey Ass'n., summer of 1972.

MIKITA, STANLEY
Born, Sokolce, Czechoslovakia, May 20, 1940
Center. Shoots right, 5'9", 165 lbs.
Last amateur club: St. Catharines (Jrs.).

Season	Club	Lea	Regular Schedule					Playoffs				
			GP	G	A	TP	PIM	GP	G	A	TP	PIM
1958-59	Chicago	NHL	3	0	1	1	4	—	—	—	—	—
1959-60	Chicago	NHL	67	8	18	26	119	3	0	1	1	2
1960-61	Chicago	NHL	66	19	34	53	100	12	*6	5	11	21
1961-62	Chicago	NHL	70	25	52	77	97	12	6	*14	*21	19
1962-63	Chicago	NHL	65	31	45	76	69	6	3	2	5	2
1963-64a	Chicago	NHL	70	39	50	*89	146	1	3	6	9	8
1964-65a	Chicago	NHL	70	28	*59	*87	154	14	3	7	10	*53
1965-66	Chicago	NHL	68	30	*48	78	58	6	1	2	3	2
1966-67abc	Chicago	NHL	70	35	*62	*97	12	6	2	2	4	2
1967-68abc	Chicago	NHL	72	40	47	*87	14	11	5	7	12	6
1968-69	Chicago	NHL	74	30	67	97	52	—	—	—	—	—
1969-70	Chicago	NHL	76	39	47	86	50	8	4	6	10	2
1970-71	Chicago	NHL	74	24	48	72	85	18	5	13	18	16
1971-72	Chicago	NHL	74	26	39	65	46	8	3	1	4	4
	NHL Totals		919	374	617	991	1006	111	41	67	108	137

a Art Ross Trophy.
b Hart Trophy.
c Lady Byng Trophy.

ORR, ROBERT GORDON (BOBBY)

Born, Parry Sound, Ont., March 20, 1948.
Defense. Shoots left. 5'11", 185 lbs.
Last amateur club: Oshawa Generals (Jrs.)

Season	Club	Lea	GP	G	A	TP	PIM	GP	G	A	TP	PIM
					Regular Schedule					Playoffs		
1966-67a	Boston	NHL	61	13	28	41	102	—	—	—	—	—
1967-68b	Boston	NHL	46	11	20	31	63	4	0	2	2	2
1968-69b	Boston	NHL	67	21	43	64	133	10	1	7	8	10
1969-70befg	Boston	NHL	76	33	*87	*120	125	14	9	11	20	14
1970-71bcdfh	Boston	NHL	78	37	*102	139	91	7	5	7	12	25
1971-72bfg	Boston	NHL	76	37	80	117	106	15	5	*19	24	19
	NHL Totals		404	152	360	512	620	50	20	46	66	70

a Won Calder Memorial Trophy.
b Won James Norris Memorial Trophy.
c NHL record for goals in regular season by a defenseman.
d NHL record for assists in regular season.
e Won Art Ross Trophy.
f Won Hart Trophy.
g Won Conn Smythe Trophy.
h Won Lou Marsh Trophy as Top Canadian Athlete.

PARK, DOUGLAS BRADFORD (BRAD)

Born, Toronto, Ont., July 6, 1948
Defense. Shoots left. 6', 190 lbs.
Last amateur club: Toronto Marlboros (Jrs.)

Season	Club	Lea	GP	G	A	TP	PIM	GP	G	A	TP	PIM
					Regular Schedule					Playoffs		
1968-69	Buffalo	AHL	17	2	12	14	49	—	—	—	—	—
1968-69	NY Rangers	NHL	54	3	23	26	70	4	0	2	2	7
1969-70	NY Rangers	NHL	60	11	26	37	98	5	1	2	3	11
1970-71	NY Rangers	NHL	60	7	37	44	114	13	0	4	4	42
1971-72	NY Rangers	NHL	75	24	49	73	130	16	4	7	11	21
	NHL Totals		257	45	135	180	412	38	5	15	20	81

RATELLE, JOSEPH GILBERT YVON JEAN

Born, Lac St. Jean, Que., October 3, 1940.
Center. Shoots left. 6'1", 175 lbs.
Last amateur club: Guelph Royals (Jrs.)

Season	Club	Lea	Regular Schedule					Playoffs				
			GP	G	A	TP	PIM	GP	G	A	TP	PIM
1959-60	Three Rivers	EPHL	3	3	5	8	0	4	0	3	3	0
1960-61	NY Rangers	NHL	3	2	1	3	0	—	—	—	—	—
1961-62	NY Rangers	NHL	31	4	8	12	4	—	—	—	—	—
1961-62	Kitch.-Waterloo	EPHL	32	10	29	39	8	7	2	6	8	2
1962-63	NY Rangers	NHL	48	11	9	20	8	—	—	—	—	—
1962-63	Baltimore	AHL	20	11	8	19	0	3	0	0	0	0
1963-64	Baltimore	AHL	57	20	26	46	2	—	—	—	—	—
1963-64	NY Rangers	NHL	15	0	7	7	6	—	—	—	—	—
1964-65	Baltimore	AHL	8	9	4	13	6	—	—	—	—	—
1964-65	NY Rangers	NHL	54	14	21	35	14	—	—	—	—	—
1965-66	NY Rangers	NHL	67	21	30	51	10	—	—	—	—	—
1966-67	NY Rangers	NHL	41	6	5	11	4	4	0	0	0	2
1967-68	NY Rangers	NHL	74	32	46	78	18	6	0	4	4	2
1968-69	NY Rangers	NHL	75	32	46	78	26	4	1	0	1	0
1969-70	NY Rangers	NHL	75	32	42	74	28	6	1	3	4	0
1970-71a	NY Rangers	NHL	78	26	46	72	14	13	2	9	11	8
1971-72b	NY Rangers	NHL	63	46	63	109	4	6	0	1	1	0
	NHL Totals		624	226	324	550	136	39	4	17	21	12

a Won Bill Masterton Memorial Trophy.
b Won Lady Byng Trophy.

WALTON, MICHAEL ROBERT (MIKE)

Born, Kirkland Lake, Ont., January 3, 1945.
Center. Shootes left. 5'9". 170 lbs.
Last amateur club: Toronto Marlboros (Jrs.)

Season	Club	Lea	Regular Schedule					Playoffs				
			GP	G	A	TP	PIM	GP	G	A	TP	PIM
1963-64	Rochester	AHL	2	0	0	0	0	—	—	—	—	—
1964-65a	Tulsa	CPHL	68	40	44	84	86	12	7	6	13	16
1965-66	Toronto	NHL	6	1	3	4	0	—	—	—	—	—
1965-66b	Rochester	AHL	68	35	51	86	67	12	*8	4	*12	*43
1966-67	Rochester	AHL	36	19	33	52	28	—	—	—	—	—
1966-67	Toronto	NHL	31	7	10	17	13	12	4	3	7	2
1967-68	Toronto	NHL	73	30	29	59	48	—	—	—	—	—
1968-69	Toronto	NHL	66	22	21	43	34	4	0	0	0	4
1969-70	Toronto	NHL	58	21	34	55	68	—	—	—	—	—
1970-71	Toronto	NHL	23	3	10	13	21	—	—	—	—	—
	Boston	NHL	22	3	5	8	10	5	2	0	2	19
1971-72	Boston	NHL	76	28	28	56	45	15	6	6	12	13
	NHL Totals		355	115	140	255	239	36	12	9	21	38

a Won CPHL Rookie Award.
b Won Dudley (Red) Garrett Memorial Trophy.
Traded to Philadelphia by Toronto with Bruce Gamble and Toronto's first
choice (Pierre Plante) in the 1971 Amateur Draft for Bernie Parent and Philadelphia's second choice (Rick Kehoe) in same draft, February 1, 1971. Philadelphia then traded Walton to Boston for Danny Schock and Rick MacLeish,
also February 1, 1971.